GOOD AND NOT EVIL IS THE UNIVERSE

GOOD AND NOT EVIL IS THE UNIVERSE

*Recurring Themes
in the Writings of George MacDonald*

Randall T. Wert

RESOURCE *Publications* • Eugene, Oregon

GOOD AND NOT EVIL IS THE UNIVERSE
Recurring Themes in the Writings of George MacDonald

Copyright © 2025 Randall T. Wert. All rights reserved. Except for brief quotations in critical publications or reviews, no part of this book may be reproduced in any manner without prior written permission from the publisher. Write: Permissions, Wipf and Stock Publishers, 199 W. 8th Ave., Suite 3, Eugene, OR 97401.

Resource Publications
An Imprint of Wipf and Stock Publishers
199 W. 8th Ave., Suite 3
Eugene, OR 97401

www.wipfandstock.com

PAPERBACK ISBN: 979-8-3852-6291-5
HARDCOVER ISBN: 979-8-3852-6292-2
EBOOK ISBN: 979-8-3852-6293-9

Contents

Preface vii
1 The Nature of God 1
2 Creation 6
3 The Uniqueness of Each Individual's Relationship with God 11
4 Suffering and Hardship 14
5 Ultimate Joy After Sorrow 19
6 The Primary Importance of Doing God's Will 28
7 Spiritual Development 33
8 Faith 57
9 Hope 67
10 Love 70
11 Repentance, Forgiveness, and Salvation 73
12 A General Disdain for Wealth and High Social Status 81
13 Nature as the Best Place to Worship 85
14 The Place of Animals in God's Kingdom 87
15 Diversity 92
Selected Works of George MacDonald 95
Subject Index 99
Scripture Index 103

Preface

My purpose in writing this book was to highlight those ideas that occur repeatedly in the works of George MacDonald. It is based most heavily on MacDonald's *Unspoken Sermons*, but in the course of my research I read every word of MacDonald's that was freely available on the Project Gutenberg website.

This is not intended to present MacDonald's ideas as a new doctrine or theology. In fact, I think he would have been horrified to find someone treating his writings in such a way. He always placed much more importance on *doing* the right thing than on *believing* the right thing.

Many people have found, and continue to find, encouragement in MacDonald's writings. Some go so far as to say that MacDonald has saved their lives from existential depression or the hopelessness inherent in the contradictions of Calvinism.

It might be surprising to find such powerful encouragement coming from a man who lost four children during his lifetime. George MacDonald was a man well acquainted with sorrow and grief. One section of this book is devoted to depression, or sorrow more generally, including the sorrow of mourning. I was loath to omit anything from this section, in the hope that any of MacDonald's insights might be helpful to someone.

One of MacDonald's uplifting messages is that good will ultimately triumph over evil:

- Near the end of *Phantastes*, the narrator states, "I know that good is coming to me—that good is always coming; though

Preface

few have at all times the simplicity and the courage to believe it."[1]

- In *David Elginbrod*, MacDonald assures us, "Love shall conquer hate; and God will overcome sin."[2]
- In *Lilith: A Romance*, Adam tells Lilith, "Good and not Evil is the Universe."[3]

Please understand the use of male nouns and pronouns in the context of the time in which these works were written. Consider this in the light of MacDonald's frequent description of God as encompassing male and female elements and his remarks on the subjugation of women in his comments on Jesus's words in Luke 4:14–21:

> What a gracious speech, what a daring pledge to a world whelmed in tyranny and wrong! To the women of it, I imagine, it sounded the sweetest, in them woke the highest hopes. They had scarce had a hearing when the Lord came; and thereupon things began to mend with them, and are mending still, for the Lord is at work, and will be. He is the refuge of the oppressed.[4]

I offer my observations in the hope that readers will discover for themselves the liberating and encouraging messages that George MacDonald has to offer.

Lenhartsville, Pennsylvania
September 2025

---

1. *Phantastes*, ch. 25.
2. *David Elginbrod*, bk. 3, ch. 24.
3. *Lilith*, ch. 29.
4. "Jesus and His Fellow Townsmen" in *Hope of the Gospel*.

1

The Nature of God:
An Absolute, Perfect Love

MANY OF MACDONALD'S CHARACTERS suffer (quite literally) from misconceptions of God. These mistaken ideas often result from the ways in which God is misrepresented by established theologies. Some of these mistaken characters eventually enjoy the benefit of learning from more enlightened persons. For example, in *There and Back*, Richard is introduced by Barbara to "a being to call God, who was a delight to think of, a being concerning whom the great negation was that of everything Richard had hitherto associated with the word God."[1]

Human limitations also prevent us from comprehending God's greatness. In *Hope of the Gospel* MacDonald points out that "there are not a few, who would be indignant at having their belief in God questioned, who yet seem greatly to fear imagining him better than he is: whether is it he or themselves they dread injuring by expecting too much of him?"[2]

If we are so prone to misunderstanding God, then how should we understand him? MacDonald touches on many aspects of God's nature in various writings, but these are perhaps best summarized

---

1. *There and Back*, ch. 23.
2. "Hope of the Universe" in *Hope of the Gospel*.

by a passage from *Dish of Orts*, in which MacDonald states that "at the heart of things and causing them to be, at the centre of monad, of world, of protoplastic mass, of loving dog, and of man most cruel, is an absolute, perfect love."³ Essential love entails essential forgiveness, as "it is God's chosen nature to forgive . . . he is bound in his own divinely willed nature to forgive."⁴ The following paragraphs highlight some other specific aspects of God's nature as presented by MacDonald.

Despite his traditional use of male pronouns in reference to God, MacDonald clearly portrays him as encompassing both male and female elements. This is plainly seen in *Adela Cathcart*, in which MacDonald refers to God as "Him who is Father and Mother both in one."⁵ In *Warlock o'Glenwarlock*, the laird tells his son Cosmo, "You can't keep true to your mother, except you remember Him who is father and mother both to all of us."⁶ In *Within and Without: A Dramatic Poem* we read,

> She is the offspring of thy beauty, God;
> Yea of the womanhood that dwells in thee:
> Thou wilt restore her to my very soul.⁷

An important—and easily misconstrued—concept is God as a *consuming fire* of purification. There are allusions to this concept in various works (e.g., *Adela Cathcart*, *Lilith*, and *Hope of the Gospel*). But it is most directly and fully developed in *Unspoken Sermons*, where it is presented as a fire that consumes all within us that cannot persist eternally: "For that which cannot be shaken shall remain. That which is immortal in God shall remain in man. The death that is in them shall be consumed. . . . Escape is hopeless. For Love is inexorable. Our God is a consuming fire."⁸

---

3. "Sketch of Individual Development" in *Dish of Orts*.
4. "Justice" in *Unspoken Sermons*, ser. 3.
5. *Adela Cathcart*, vol. 2, ch. 2.
6. *Warlock o' Glenwarlock*, ch. 3.
7. *Within and Without*, pt. 4, sc. 13, in *Poetical Works*, vol. 1.
8. "Consuming Fire" in *Unspoken Sermons*, ser. 1.

Lest the reader confuse this consuming fire with the eternal damnation so often preached as fire-and-brimstone, it is best to let MacDonald explain for himself what he actually means:

> The fire of God, which is his essential being, his love, his creative power, is a fire unlike its earthly symbol in this, that it is only at a distance it burns—that the farther from him, it burns the worse, and that when we turn and begin to approach him, the burning begins to change to comfort, which comfort will grow to such bliss that the heart at length cries out with a gladness no other gladness can reach.... When the man yields his self and all that self's low world, and returns to his lord and God, then that which, before, he was aware of only as burning, he will feel as love, comfort, strength—an eternal, ever-growing life in him.[9]

In keeping with his universalism, MacDonald refers to the final fuel for this fire: "But at length, O God, wilt thou not cast Death and Hell into the lake of Fire—even into thine own consuming self? Death shall then die everlastingly."[10]

The nature of God as one who does not conceal, but reveals, is reflected in Christ's mission on earth. For one thing, Christ reveals the Father to us: "The Holy Child, the Son of the Father, has nothing to conceal, but all the Godhead to reveal."[11] "It was not for himself he came to the world—not to establish his own power over the doings, his own influence over the hearts of men: he came that they might know the Father who was his joy, his life."[12] "The mission undertaken by the Son was not to show himself as having all power in heaven and earth, but to reveal his Father, to show him to men such as he is, that men may know him, and knowing, trust him."[13]

In *Hope of the Gospel* MacDonald explains further:

---

9. "Fear of God" in *Unspoken Sermons*, ser. 2.
10. "Consuming Fire" in *Unspoken Sermons*, ser. 1.
11. "Eloi" in *Unspoken Sermons*, ser. 1.
12. "Way" in *Unspoken Sermons*, ser. 2.
13. "Cause of Spiritual Stupidity" in *Unspoken Sermons*, ser. 2.

> The Father knows the Son and sends him to us that we may know him; the Son knows the Father, and dies to reveal him. The glory of God's mysteries is—that they are for his children to look into.... No man, when first he comes to himself, can have any true knowledge of God; he can only have a desire after such knowledge. But while he does not know him at all, he cannot become in his heart God's child; so the Father must draw nearer to him. He sends therefore his first born, who does know him, is exactly like him, and can represent him perfectly. Drawn to him, the children receive him, and then he is able to reveal the Father to them.[14]

Of course, Christ also came to be an example for us to follow, as MacDonald discusses in *Unspoken Sermons*: "He had been amongst his brethren what he would have his brethren be. He had done for them what he would have them do for God and for each other."[15] "When he says, 'Take my yoke upon you,' he does not mean a yoke which he would lay upon our shoulders; it is his own yoke he tells us to take, and to learn of him—it is the yoke he is himself carrying, the yoke his perfect Father had given him to carry. The will of the Father is the yoke he would have us take, and bear also with him."[16]

MacDonald emphasizes that Christ's mission was to bring us, God's children, back to our Father. This is expressed several times in *Unspoken Sermons*:

- "I believe that Jesus Christ *is* our atonement; that through him we are reconciled to, made one with God."[17]
- "He brings and is bringing God and man, and man and man, into perfect unity: 'I in them and thou in me, that they may be made perfect in one.'"[18]

---

14. "Yoke of Jesus" in *Hope of the Gospel*.
15. "Hands of the Father" in *Unspoken Sermons*, ser. 1.
16. "Self-Denial" in *Unspoken Sermons*, ser. 2.
17. "Justice" in *Unspoken Sermons*, ser. 3.
18. "Justice" in *Unspoken Sermons*, ser. 3.

- "Never could we have known the heart of the Father, never felt it possible to love him as sons, but for him who cast himself into the gulf that yawned between us."[19]

In *Salted with Fire*, MacDonald describes a similar insight gained by the character Maggie: "Now she understood the heart of the Son of Man, come to find and carry back the stray children to their Father and His."[20]

Various aspects of the purpose and meaning of Christ's death are also explored in *Unspoken Sermons*: "The Lord did not die to provide a man with the wretched heaven he may invent for himself, or accept invented for him by others; he died to give him life, and bring him to the heaven of the Father's peace; the children must share in the essential bliss of the Father and the Son."[21] "Repentance, restitution, confession, prayer for forgiveness, righteous dealing thereafter, is the sole possible, the only true make-up for sin. For nothing less than this did Christ die. . . . I believe that he died to deliver me from all meanness, all pretence, all falseness, all unfairness, all poverty of spirit, all cowardice, all fear, all anxiety, all forms of self-love, all trust or hope in possession; to make me merry as a child, the child of our father in heaven, loving nothing but what is lovely, desiring nothing I should be ashamed to let the universe of God see me desire."[22] And in *Hope of the Gospel* MacDonald adds, "The lord of life died that his father's children might grow perfect in love—might love their brothers and sisters as he loved them."[23]

---

19. "Abba, Father!" in *Unspoken Sermons*, ser. 2.
20. *Salted with Fire*, ch. 5.
21. "Truth in Jesus" in *Unspoken Sermons*, ser. 2.
22. "Justice" in *Unspoken Sermons*, ser. 3.
23. "Sorrow the Pledge of Joy" in *Hope of the Gospel*.

2

Creation: *Loved into Being*

IN *SALTED WITH FIRE*, MacDonald refers to God's imagination as being "at once the birth and the very truth of everything."[1] In *There and Back*, he asserts that we do not "come of God's intellect, but of his imagination."[2] In a similar vein, MacDonald states that "all live things were thoughts to begin with"[3] and that "man is but a thought of God."[4]

MacDonald also sees creation as an ongoing, eternal labor of God's love. In *Unspoken Sermons* he explains: "God is life, and the will-source of life. In the outflowing of that life, I know him; and when I am told that he is love, I see that if he were not love he would not, could not create. I know nothing deeper in him than love, nor believe there is in him anything deeper than love—nay, that there can be anything deeper than love. The being of God is love, therefore creation. I imagine that from all eternity he has been creating . . . to make other beings—beings like us, I imagine the labour of a God, an eternal labour."[5] In *There and Back*, we read that "He did not make us with his hands, but loved us out of

1. *Salted with Fire*, ch. 4.
2. *There and Back*, ch. 54.
3. *Lilith*, ch. 5.
4. "Imagination: Its Function and Its Culture" in *Dish of Orts*.
5. "Life" in *Unspoken Sermons*, ser. 2.

his heart."⁶ And in *Lilith* Mr. Raven explains that "love, not hate, is deepest in what Love 'loved into being.'"⁷

In *Unspoken Sermons* MacDonald envisions a joyous culmination of the agonizing process of creation for each individual: "The whole history is a divine agony to give divine life to creatures. The outcome of that agony, the victory of that creative and again creative energy, will be radiant life, whereof joy unspeakable is the flower. Every child will look in the eyes of the Father, and the eyes of the Father will receive the child with an infinite embrace."⁸

A further implication of creation is our dependence on God. He has made us in such a way that we need him, and we therefore have a natural claim upon him and his help. This idea is thoroughly discussed in *Unspoken Sermons*:

- "It is God to whom every hunger, every aspiration, every desire, every longing of our nature is to be referred; he made all our needs—made us the creatures of a thousand necessities—and have we no claim on him? Nay, we have claims innumerable, infinite; and his one great claim on us is that we should claim our claims of him."⁹

- "What can please the father of men better than to hear his child cry to him from whom he came, 'Here I am, O God! Thou hast made me: give me that which thou hast made me needing.' The child's necessity, his weakness, his helplessness, are the strongest of all his claims."¹⁰

- "What if the good of all our smaller and lower needs lies in this, that they help to drive us to God?"¹¹

- "What is there for us, what can we think of, what do, but go to God?—what but go to him with this our own difficulty

---

6. *There and Back*, ch. 54.
7. *Lilith*, ch. 17.
8. "Life" in *Unspoken Sermons*, ser. 2.
9. "Voice of Job" in *Unspoken Sermons*, ser. 2.
10. "Voice of Job" in *Unspoken Sermons*, ser. 2.
11. "Word of Jesus on Prayer" in *Unspoken Sermons*, ser. 2.

and need? And where is the natural refuge, there must be the help. There can be no need for which he has no supply. The best argument that he has help, is that we have need."[12]

MacDonald also addresses this theme in *Within and Without: A Dramatic Poem*:

> Have I no claim on thee? True, I have none
> That springs from me, but much that springs from thee.
> Hast thou not made me? Liv'st thou not in me?
> I have done naught for thee, am but a want;
> But thou who art rich in giving, canst give claims;
> And this same need of thee which thou hast given,
> Is a strong claim on thee to give thyself,
> And makes me bold to rise and come to thee.[13]

This view of our claims on God naturally has implications for our communication with him. MacDonald has much to say on this topic, as well. *Unspoken Sermons* proposes that our relationship to God and our claims on him suggest that we should approach him boldly in prayer, without fearing that we might ask for the wrong things:

> If there be a God, and I am his creature, there may be, there should be, there must be some communication open between him and me. . . . Shall I not tell him that I need him to comfort me? his breath to move upon the face of the waters of the Chaos he has made? Shall I not cry to him to be in me rest and strength? to quiet this uneasy motion called life, and make me live indeed? to deliver me from my sins, and make me clean and glad? Such a cry is of the child to the Father: if there be a Father, verily he will hear, and let the child know that he hears! Every need of God, lifting up the heart, is a seeking of God, is a begging for himself, is profoundest prayer, and the root and inspirer of all other prayer. . . . Communion with God is the one need of the soul beyond all other need; prayer is the beginning of that communion, and

---

12. "Man's Difficulty Concerning Prayer" in *Unspoken Sermons*, ser. 2.
13. *Within and Without*, pt. 1, sc. 3, in *Poetical Works*, vol. 1.

some need is the motive of that prayer. . . . So begins a communion, a talking with God, a coming-to-one with him, which is the sole end of prayer, yea, of existence itself in its infinite phases. . . . Surely it is better and more trusting to tell him all without fear or anxiety. Was it not thus the Lord carried himself towards his Father? . . . There is no apprehension that God might be displeased with him for saying what he would like. . . . Neither did he regard his Father's plans as necessarily so fixed that they could not be altered to his prayer. The true son-faith is that which comes with boldness, fearless of the Father doing anything but what is right fatherly, patient, and full of loving-kindness. . . . The true child will not fear, but lay bare his wishes to the perfect Father. The Father may will otherwise, but his grace will be enough for the child.[14]

In *Hope of the Gospel* we find the same idea expressed more concisely: "One thing is clear in regard to every trouble—that the natural way with it is straight to the Father's knee. The Father is father *for* his children, else why did he make himself their father?"[15]

MacDonald asserts that the answers we receive to our prayers might not be exactly what we immediately desire. "Yet is every prayer heard; and the real soul of the prayer may require, for its real answer, that it should not be granted in the form in which it is requested. . . . If it be granted that any answer which did not come of love, and was not for the final satisfaction of him who prayed, would be unworthy of God; that it is the part of love and knowledge to watch over the wayward, ignorant child; then the trouble of seemingly unanswered prayers begins to abate, and a lovely hope and comfort takes its place in the child-like soul."[16] "We must not tie God to our measures of time, or think he has forgotten that prayer even which, apparently unanswered, we have forgotten."[17]

In similar language in *The Miracles of Our Lord*, MacDonald points out that prayer is answered in the way that is best for the

---

14. "Word of Jesus on Prayer" in *Unspoken Sermons*, ser. 2.
15. "Sorrow the Pledge of Joy" in *Hope of the Gospel*.
16. "Word of Jesus on Prayer" in *Unspoken Sermons*, ser. 2.
17. "Man's Difficulty Concerning Prayer" in *Unspoken Sermons*, ser. 2.

person, not necessarily in the way that the person has requested: "God has not to satisfy the judgment of men as they are, but as they will be and must be, having learned the high and perfectly honest and grand way of things which is his will. For God to give men just what they want would often be the same as for a man to give gin to the night-wanderer whom he had it in his power to take home and set to work for wages."[18]

Always one to encourage others, MacDonald urges us to continue praying: "It looks as if he did not hear you: never mind; he does; it must be that he does; go on as the [persistent widow of the parable in Luke] did; you too will be heard. She is heard at last, and in virtue of her much going; God hears at once, and will avenge speedily."[19]

MacDonald also has much to say about prayer in chapter 38 of *Paul Faber, Surgeon*.

---

18. *Miracles of Our Lord*, ch. 5.
19. "Word of Jesus on Prayer" in *Unspoken Sermons*, ser. 2.

3

The Uniqueness of Each Individual's Relationship with God: *The White Stone with the New Name*

MACDONALD REPEATEDLY ASSERTS THAT each individual's relationship with God is unique. The strongest statements of this view are found in *Unspoken Sermons*:

- "The Spirit has a revelation for every man individually."[1]
- "If I did not believe in a special inspiration to every man who asks for the holy spirit, the good thing of God, I should have to throw aside the whole tale as an imposture; for the Lord has, according to that tale, promised such inspiration to those who ask it."[2]
- "Every man, woman, child—for the incomplete also is his, and in its very incompleteness reveals him as a progressive worker in his creation—is a revealer of God. I have my message of my great Lord, you have yours."[3]

---

1. "Higher Faith" in *Unspoken Sermons*, ser. 1.
2. "Knowing of the Son" in *Unspoken Sermons*, ser. 3.
3. "Inheritance" in *Unspoken Sermons*, ser. 3.

- "Every one of us is something that the other is not, and therefore knows some thing—it may be without knowing that he knows it—which no one else knows; and that it is every one's business, as one of the kingdom of light, and inheritor in it all, to give his portion to the rest; for we are one family, with God at the head and the heart of it, and Jesus Christ, our elder brother, teaching us of the Father, whom he only knows."[4]

This uniqueness is also reflected in Jesus's miracles of healing: "I may not find a better place for remarking on the variety of our Lord's treatment of those whom he cured; that is, the variety of the form in which he conveyed the cure. In the record I do not think we find two cases treated in the same manner. There is no massing of the people with him. In his behaviour to men, just as in their relation to his Father, every man is alone with him."[5]

For MacDonald, this concept is also embodied in the "white stone with a new name" mentioned in Rev 2:17. MacDonald expounds on this in *Unspoken Sermons*: "The mystic symbol [i.e., the white stone] has for its centre of significance the fact of the personal individual relation of every man to his God."[6] "The true name is one which expresses the character, the nature, the being, the *meaning* of the person who bears it. It is the man's own symbol,—his soul's picture, in a word,—the sign which belongs to him and to no one else. Who can give a man this, his own name? God alone. For no one but God sees what the man is, or even, seeing what he is, could express in a name-word the sum and harmony of what he sees."[7] "The name is one 'which no man knoweth saving he that receiveth it.' Not only then has each man his individual relation to God, but each man has his peculiar relation to God. He is to God a peculiar being, made after his own fashion, and that of no one else; for when he is perfected he shall receive the new name which no one else can understand. Hence he can worship God as

---

4. "Inheritance" in *Unspoken Sermons*, ser. 3.
5. *Miracles of Our Lord*, ch. 5.
6. "New Name" in *Unspoken Sermons*, ser. 1.
7. "New Name" in *Unspoken Sermons*, ser. 1.

Each Individual's Relationship with God

no man else can worship him,—can understand God as no man else can understand him."[8] "As the fir-tree lifts up itself with a far different need from the need of the palm-tree, so does each man stand before God, and lift up a different humanity to the common Father. And for each God has a different response. With every man he has a secret—the secret of the new name."[9]

In *Lilith* the mysterious Cat-woman tells the narrator that "hardly any one anywhere knows his own name! It would make many a fine gentleman stare to hear himself addressed by what is really his name!"[10] This topic is also addressed in stanza 22 of "The Disciple" from *Poetical Works*, vol. 1.

---

8. "New Name" in *Unspoken Sermons*, ser. 1.
9. "New Name" in *Unspoken Sermons*, ser. 1.
10. *Lilith*, ch. 15

4

Suffering and Hardship:
The Orderly Arrangement of Our Trials

BEFORE OFFERING AN EXPLANATION of the inevitability and purposes of suffering, MacDonald acknowledges that it is all "against the ideal order of things. No man can love pain. It is an unlovely, an ugly, abhorrent thing. The more true and delicate the bodily and mental constitution, the more must it recoil from pain. No one, I think, could dislike pain so much as the Saviour must have disliked it. God dislikes it. He is then on our side in the matter. He knows it is grievous to be borne, a thing he would cast out of his blessed universe, save for reasons.... While [God's children] suffer he is brooding over them an eternal day, suffering with them but rejoicing in their future."[1]

In *Marquis of Lossie*, Malcolm explains to Clementina that God suffers with us, as reflected by Christ's suffering, and also sustains us in our suffering. In *Hope of the Gospel* MacDonald asserts,

> The poor, the hungry, the weeping, the hated, may lament their lot as if God had forgotten them; but God is all the time caring for them. Blessed in his sight now, they shall soon know themselves blessed. "Blessed are ye that weep now, for ye shall laugh."—Welcome words

1. *Miracles of Our Lord*, ch. 3.

from the glad heart of the Saviour! Do they not make our hearts burn within us?—They shall be comforted even to laughter! The poor, the hungry, the weeping, the hated, the persecuted, are the powerful, the opulent, the merry, the loved, the victorious of God's kingdom,—to be filled with good things, to laugh for very delight, to be honoured and sought and cherished![2]

Sometimes we are not sure of how we manage to endure a difficult time and only sense in retrospect that God's power, as manifested in nature and in those around us, has seen us through it. In *Thomas Wingfold, Curate*, MacDonald writes of the title character's crisis of faith, "How he got through the Sunday he never could have told. What times a man may get through—he knows not how!"[3] MacDonald continues,

> He thought afterwards, when the time had passed, that surely in this period of darkness he had been visited and upheld by a power whose presence and even influence escaped his consciousness. He knew not how else he could have got through it. Also he remembered that strange helps had come to him; that the aspects of nature then wonderfully softened towards him, that then first he began to feel sympathy with her ways and shows, and to see in them all the working of a diffused humanity. He remembered how once a hawthorn bud set him weeping; and how once, as he went miserable to church, a child looked up in his face and smiled, and how in the strength of that smile he had walked boldly to the lectern.[4]

MacDonald suggests that "there are as much Providence and mercy in the orderly arrangement of our trials as in their inevitable arrival."[5] In various writings he attempts to show the purpose and even benefits of the hardships experienced by his characters:

---

2. "Reward of Obedience" in *Hope of the Gospel*.
3. *Thomas Wingfold*, vol. 1, ch. 12.
4. *Thomas Wingfold*, vol. 1, ch. 12.
5. *Far Above Rubies*.

- "People must have troubles, else would they grow unendurable for pride and insolence."[6]
- "The intellect, great thing though it be, is yet but the soil out of which, or rather in which, higher things must grow, and it is well when that soil is not too strong, so to speak, for the most gracious and lovely of plants to root themselves in it. When the said soil is proud and unwilling to serve, it must be thinned and pulverized with sickness, failure, poverty, fear—that the good seeds of God's garden may be able to root themselves in it; when they get up a little, they will use all the riches and all the strength of the stiffest soil."[7]
- "One thing is clear, that poor Juliet, like most women, and more men, would never have begun to learn any thing worth learning, if she had not been brought into genuine, downright trouble. Indeed I am not sure but some of those who seem so good as to require no trouble, are just those who have already been most severely tried."[8]
- "There are thousands for whom a blow is a better thing than expostulation, persuasion, or any sort of kindness. They are such that nothing but a blow will set their door ajar for love to get in. That is why hardships, troubles, disappointments, and all kinds of pain and suffering, are sent to so many of us. We are so full of ourselves, and feel so grand, that we should never come to know what poor creatures we are, never begin to do better, but for the knock-down blows that the loving God gives us. We do not like them, but he does not spare us for that."[9]

A closely related topic is our freedom to choose evil or good, and the question of why God permits this freedom. MacDonald acknowledges that it is a difficult question. In *Lilith* he tells us,

---

6. *Thomas Wingfold*, vol. 2, ch. 12.
7. *Donal Grant*, ch. 83.
8. *Paul Faber*, ch. 38.
9. *Rough Shaking*, ch. 23.

"None but God hates evil and understands it."[10] In *Sir Gibbie* we read, "There is a bewilderment about the very nature of evil which only he who made us capable of evil that we might be good, can comprehend."[11]

In *Unspoken Sermons* MacDonald sets forth his explanation of why God does not force us to choose the good: "The truth is this: He wants to make us in his own image, *choosing the good, refusing* the evil. How should he effect this if he were *always* moving us from within, as he does at divine intervals, towards the beauty of holiness? God gives us room *to be*; does not oppress us with his will; 'stands away from us,' that we may act from ourselves, that we may exercise the pure will for good."[12] Free will also creates a stronger bond with God. He "made our *apartness* from himself, that freedom should bind us divinely dearer to himself; . . . the freer the man, the stronger the bond that binds him to him who made his freedom."[13]

In *Salted with Fire*, a reformed James Blatherwick comes to recognize the ultimate good that God has brought forth from James's former evil behavior, explaining to his wife:

> Ignorant creatures go about asking why God permits evil: *we* know why! It may be He could with a word cause evil to cease—but would that be to create good? The word might make us good like oxen or harmless sheep, but would that be a goodness worthy of him who was made in the image of God? If a man ceased to be *capable* of evil, he must cease to be a man! What would the goodness be that could not help being good—that had no choice in the matter, but must be such because it was so made? God chooses to be good, else he would not be God: man must choose to be good, else he cannot be the son of God! Herein we see the grand love of the Father of men—that he gives them a share, and that share as necessary as his own, in the making of themselves! Thus, and

---

10. *Lilith*, ch. 39.
11. *Sir Gibbie*, ch. 41.
12. "Eloi" in *Unspoken Sermons*, ser. 1.
13. "Eloi" in *Unspoken Sermons*, ser. 1.

thus only, that is, by willing the good, can they become "partakers of the divine nature!"[14]

Ultimately, even evil is turned to good purposes, according to MacDonald. His narrator in *Phantastes* concludes the book by commenting, "What we call evil, is the only and best shape, which, for the person and his condition at the time, could be assumed by the best good."[15] In *Weighed and Wanting*, MacDonald explains, "The good of all evil is to make a way for love, which is essential good. Therefore evil exists, and will exist until love destroy and cast it out."[16]

---

14. *Salted with Fire*, ch. 26.
15. *Phantastes*, ch. 25.
16. *Weighed and Wanting*, ch. 50.

5

Ultimate Joy After Sorrow:
The Comfort That Is Drawing Nigh

FOR MACDONALD, SORROW IS temporary, while joy is everlasting. "The sorrows are sickly things and die, while the joys are strong divine children, and shall live for evermore."[1] "The 'glad creator' never made man for sorrow: it is but a stormy strait through which he must pass to his ocean of peace. He 'makes the joy the last in every song.'"[2]

In *Warlock o'Glenwarlock*, we read,

> Shall we then bemoan any darkness? Shall we not rather gird up our strength to encounter it, that we too from our side may break the passage for the light beyond? He who fights with the dark shall know the gentleness that makes man great—the dawning countenance of the God of hope. But that was not for Cosmo just yet. The night must fulfill its hours. Men are meant and sent to be troubled—that they may rise above the whole region of storm, above all possibility of being troubled.[3]

---

1. *Mary Marston*, ch. 56.
2. "Sorrow the Pledge of Joy" in *Hope of the Gospel*.
3. *Warlock o' Glenwarlock*, ch. 36.

This eternal joy may apply especially to those who mourn for lost loved ones. In *Hope of the Gospel* MacDonald writes,

> No man will carry his mourning with him into heaven—or, if he does, it will speedily be turned either into joy, or into what will result in joy, namely, redemptive action. . . . It may give pleasure to know that the promise of comfort to those that mourn, may specially apply to those that mourn because their loved have gone out of their sight, and beyond the reach of their cry. . . . I think [the Lord] congratulated the mourners upon the grief they were enduring, because he saw the excellent glory of the comfort that was drawing nigh; because he knew the immeasurably greater joy to which the sorrow was at once clearing the way and conducting the mourner.[4]

MacDonald was clearly a person who was well acquainted with depression and the deceptive nature of the feelings associated with it. Speaking as *The Vicar's Daughter*, Wynnie, MacDonald writes: "There were times when life itself seemed vanishing in an abyss of nothingness, when all my consciousness consisted in this, that I knew I was not, and when I could not believe that I should ever be restored to the well-being of existence. The worst of it was, that, in such moods, it seemed as if I had hitherto been deluding myself with rainbow fancies as often as I had been aware of blessedness, as there was, in fact, no wine of life apart from its effervescence."[5] But Wynnie goes on to state, "If I have learned any valuable lesson in my life, it is this, that no one's feelings are a measure of eternal facts."[6]

MacDonald's familiarity with depression is also shown in some of his poetry—for example, in these two entries from *The Diary of an Old Soul*:

---

4. "Sorrow the Pledge of Joy" in *Hope of the Gospel*.
5. *Vicar's Daughter*, ch. 11.
6. *Vicar's Daughter*, ch. 11.

- From February 25:

    There is a misty twilight of the soul,
    A sickly eclipse, low brooding o'er a man,
    When the poor brain is as an empty bowl,
    And the thought-spirit, weariful and wan,
    Turning from that which yet it loves the best,
    Sinks moveless, with life-poverty opprest:—
    Watch then, O Lord, thy feebly glimmering coal.[7]

- From April 20:

    God, help me, dull of heart, to trust in thee.
    Thou art the father of me—not any mood
    Can part me from the One, the verily Good.
    When fog and failure o'er my being brood.
    When life looks but a glimmering marshy clod,
    No fire out flashing from the living God—
    Then, then, to rest in faith were worthy victory![8]

In *Unspoken Sermons* MacDonald also demonstrates the insight that mentally ill people are in conflict with forces that are not part of their own true selves. He assures them that God will side with them against these evil forces that are alien to their own nature:

> The suggestion [that God will avenge us] is comforting to those whose foes are within them, for, if so, then he recognizes the evils of self, against which we fight, not as parts of ourselves, but as our foes, on which he will avenge the true self that is at strife with them. And certainly no evil is, or ever could be, of the essential being and nature of the creature God made! The thing that is not good, however associated with our being, is against that being, not of it—is its enemy, on which we need to be avenged. When we fight, he will avenge. Till we fight, evil shall have dominion over us, a dominion to make us miserable; other than miserable can no one be, under the yoke of a nature contrary to his own. Comfort thyself

---

7. "February" in *Diary of Old Soul*.
8. "April" in *Diary of Old Soul*.

then, who findest thine own heart and soul, or rather the things that move therein, too much for thee: God will avenge his own elect. He is not delaying; he is at work for thee. Only thou must pray, and not faint. Ask, ask; it shall be given you. Seek most the best things; to ask for the best things is to have them; the seed of them is in you, or you could not ask for them.[9]

In a hopeful reference to the ultimate outcome of this inner conflict, the title character of *Wilfrid Cumbermede* tells his friend Charley, "In time, of course, the angels of the heart will expel the demons of the brain."[10]

Unspoken Sermons points out that a depressed person might seem to long for death, when in fact the remedy lies in more of life itself:

> Low-sunk life imagines itself weary of life, but it is death, not life, it is weary of. Never a cry went out after the opposite of life from any soul that knew what life is. Why does the poor, worn, out-worn suicide seek death? Is it not in reality to escape from death? . . . The cure for everything must be life—that the ills which come with existence, are from its imperfection, not of itself—that what we need is more of it. We who *are*, have nothing to do with death; our relations are alone with life. . . . Let us in all the troubles of life remember—that our one lack is life—that what we need is more life—more of the life-making presence in us making us more, and more largely, alive. When most oppressed, when most weary of life, as our unbelief would phrase it, let us bethink ourselves that it is in truth the inroad and presence of death we are weary of. When most inclined to sleep, let us rouse ourselves to live. . . . He has the victory who, in the midst of pain and weakness, cries out, not for death, not for the repose of forgetfulness, but for strength to fight; for more power, more consciousness of being, more God in him.[11]
>
> Friends, those of you who know, or suspect, that these

9. "Man's Difficulty Concerning Prayer" in *Unspoken Sermons*, ser. 2.
10. *Wilfrid Cumbermede*, ch. 42.
11. "Life" in *Unspoken Sermons*, ser. 2.

things are true, let us arise and live—arise even in the darkest moments of spiritual stupidity, when hope itself sees nothing to hope for.[12]

Unspoken Sermons also emphasizes that recovery from depression might require a person to act without waiting to feel better, especially considering the deceptive nature of one's feelings in this state:

> Troubled soul, thou art not bound to feel, but thou art bound to arise. God loves thee whether thou feelest or not. Thou canst not love when thou wilt, but thou art bound to fight the hatred in thee to the last. Try not to feel good when thou art not good, but cry to Him who is good. He changes not because thou changest. Nay, he has an especial tenderness of love towards thee for that thou art in the dark and hast no light, and his heart is glad when thou dost arise and say, "I will go to my Father." For he sees thee through all the gloom through which thou canst not see him. Will thou his will. Say to him: "My God, I am very dull and low and hard; but thou art wise and high and tender, and thou art my God. I am thy child. Forsake me not." Then fold the arms of thy faith, and wait in quietness until light goes up in thy darkness. Fold the arms of thy Faith I say, but not of thy Action: bethink thee of something that thou oughtest to do, and go and do it, if it be but the sweeping of a room, or the preparing of a meal, or a visit to a friend. Heed not thy feelings: Do thy work.[13] When will once begins to aspire, it will soon find that action must precede feeling, that the man may know the foundation itself of feeling. . . . All true action clears the springs of right feeling, and lets their waters rise and flow.[14]

In various works, MacDonald shows that depression can be alleviated by escaping the "dungeon of self" and focusing instead

---

12. "Creation in Christ" in *Unspoken Sermons*, ser. 3.
13. "Eloi" in *Unspoken Sermons*, ser. 1.
14. "Love Thy Neighbour" in *Unspoken Sermons*, ser. 1.

on loving and helping others. The following examples show how he makes this point without condemning the sufferer:

- "Nor thus shall a man lose the consciousness of well-being. Far deeper and more complete, God and his neighbour will flash it back upon him—pure as life. No more will he agonize 'with sick assay' to generate it in the light of his own decadence. For he shall know the glory of his own being in the light of God and of his brother."[15]

- Wynnie, the *Vicar's Daughter*, having been always prone to depression herself, rejects its stigma as she writes of herself: "I have a hope that a too-much-thinking about yourself may not *always* be pure selfishness. It may be something else wrong in you that makes you uncomfortable, and keeps drawing your eyes towards the aching place. I will hope so till I get rid of the whole business, and then I shall not care much how it came or what it was."[16]

- "But to try to make others comfortable is the only way to get right comfortable ourselves, and that comes partly of not being able to think so much about ourselves when we are helping other people. For our Selves will always do pretty well if we don't pay them too much attention."[17]

MacDonald also shows that recognizing God as our Father is essential to moving from misery to happiness. In *Unspoken Sermons* we read, "The refusal to look up to God as our Father is the one central wrong in the whole human affair; the inability, the one central misery: whatever serves to clear any difficulty from the way of the recognition of the Father, will more or less undermine every difficulty in life. . . . Until you yourself are the [child] of God you were born to be, you will never find life a good thing."[18]

---

15. "Love Thy Neighbour" in *Unspoken Sermons*, ser. 1.
16. *Vicar's Daughter*, ch. 7.
17. *Back of North Wind*, ch. 16.
18. "Abba, Father!" in *Unspoken Sermons*, ser. 2.

Ultimate Joy After Sorrow

Unspoken Sermons also presents God as our refuge at times when we wander in the darkness of depression. "That man is perfect in faith who can come to God in the utter dearth of his feelings and his desires, without a glow or an aspiration, with the weight of low thoughts, failures, neglects, and wandering forgetfulness, and say to Him, 'Thou art my refuge, because thou art my home.'"[19] "The word of God once understood, a man must live by the faith of what God is, and not by his own feelings even in regard to God. It is the Truth itself, that which God is, known by what goeth out of his mouth, that man lives by. And when he can no longer *feel* the truth, he shall not therefore die. He lives because God is true; and he is able to know that he lives because he knows, having once understood the word, that God is truth. He believes in the God of former vision, lives by that word therefore, when all is dark and there is no vision."[20] "Let us then arise in God-born strength every time that we feel the darkness closing, or become aware that it has closed around us, and say, 'I am of the Light and not of the Darkness.'"[21] "Less than God just as he is will not comfort men for the essential sorrow of their existence. Only God the gift can turn that sorrow into essential joy: Jesus came to give them God, who is eternal life."[22]

To have faith at times when we are feeling well is easy; the strongest faith is that which occurs in defiance of the depths of depression. "Faith, in such circumstances [of depression], must be of the purest, and may be of the strongest. In few other circumstances can it have such an opportunity—can it rise to equal height. It may be its final lesson, and deepest. God is in it just in his seeming to be not in it—that we may choose him in the darkness of the feeling, stretch out the hand to him when we cannot see him, verify him in the vagueness of the dream, call to him in the absence of impulse, obey him in the weakness of the will."[23] Elsewhere MacDonald

---

19. "Child in the Midst" in *Unspoken Sermons*, ser. 1.
20. "Temptation in the Wilderness" in *Unspoken Sermons*, ser. 1.
21. "Eloi" in *Unspoken Sermons*, ser. 1.
22. "Cause of Spiritual Stupidity" in *Unspoken Sermons*, ser. 2.
23. *Weighed and Wanting*, ch. 43.

reminds us that even when crying out, "Why hast thou forsaken me?" Jesus still directed the cry to "My God!"[24]

Among other remedies for depression, MacDonald suggests the possible value of physical labor. Speaking of the character Thomas Worboise, he writes,

> His hope, however, alternated with such fits of misery and despair, that if it had not been for the bodily work he had to do, he thought he would have lost his reason. I believe not a few keep hold of their senses in virtue of doing hard work. I knew an earl's son, an heir, who did so. And I think that not a few, especially women, lose their senses just from having nothing to do. Many more, who are not in danger of this, lose their health, and more still lose their purity and rectitude. In other words, health—physical, mental, moral, and spiritual—requires, for its existence and continuance, work, often hard and bodily labor.[25]

Two excerpts from *Poetical Works* may help underscore MacDonald's familiarity with depression and his hope in positive outcomes:

- From "Hard Times":

    > But, Lord, thy child will be sad—
    > As sad as it pleases thee;
    > Will sit, not seeking to be glad,
    > Till thou bid sadness flee,
    > And, drawing near,
    > With thy good cheer
    > Awake thy life in me.[26]

- From *Within and Without: A Dramatic Poem*:

    > When on the earth I lay, crushed down beneath
    > A hopeless weight of empty desolation,
    > Thy loving face was lighted then, O Christ,

24. "Eloi" in *Unspoken Sermons*, ser. 1.
25. *Guild Court*, ch. 44.
26. "Hard Times" in *Poetical Works*, vol. 1.

Ultimate Joy After Sorrow

With expectation of my joy to come,
When all the realm of possible ill should lie
Under my feet, and I should stand as now
Heart-sure of thee, true-hearted, only One.[27]

---

27. *Within and Without*, pt. 5, sc. 3, in *Poetical Works*, vol. 1.

6

The Primary Importance of Doing God's Will: *The One Key of Life*

THE NECESSITY OF ALIGNING ourselves with God's will is the one theme that recurs most often throughout MacDonald's works. In *Unspoken Sermons* he states, "Man's first business is, 'What does God want me to do?'"[1] "If, instead of speculation, we gave ourselves to obedience, what a difference would soon be seen in the world! Oh, the multitude of so-called religious questions which the Lord would answer with, 'strive to enter in at the strait gate!' Many eat and drink and talk and teach in his presence; few do the things he says to them! Obedience is the one key of life."[2]

Christ himself modeled obedience to his Father's will as his primary concern; the yoke that he tells us to take upon us is the yoke that he himself is already bearing. In *Unspoken Sermons* we read that "to the Son of God the will of God is Life.... The Father shall order what comes next. The Son will obey.... Nothing but the obedience of the Son, the obedience unto the death, the absolute *doing* of the will of God because it was the truth, could redeem the prisoner, the widow, the orphan."[3]

1. "Temptation in the Wilderness" in *Unspoken Sermons*, ser. 1.
2. "Word of Jesus on Prayer" in *Unspoken Sermons*, ser. 2.
3. "Temptation in the Wilderness" in *Unspoken Sermons*, ser. 1.

THE PRIMARY IMPORTANCE OF DOING GOD'S WILL

Obedience to God's will is the way to life for us, as well. In *Unspoken Sermons* MacDonald explains: "When the man thus accepts his own causing life, *and sets himself to live the will of that causing life,* humbly eager after the privileges of his origin,—thus receiving God, he becomes, in the act, a partaker of the divine nature, a true son of the living God, and an heir of all he possesses: by the obedience of a son, he receives into himself the very life of the Father.... If we do the will of God, eternal life is ours."[4] "We must take the will of God as the very life of our being; we must neither try to get our own way, nor trouble ourselves as to what may be thought or said of us."[5]

Aligning our will with God's will brings freedom from slavery, as we find in various works of MacDonald. "Not any abstract truth, not all abstract truth, not truth its very metaphysical self, held by purest insight into entity, can make any man free; but the truth done, the truth loved, the truth lived by the man."[6] "But a free will is not the liberty to do whatever one likes, but the power of doing whatever one sees ought to be done, even in the very face of otherwise overwhelming impulse. There lies freedom indeed."[7] "There is no slave but the creature that wills against its creator."[8] "It is vain to think that any weariness, however caused, any burden, however slight, may be got rid of otherwise than by bowing the neck to the yoke of the Father's will. There can be no other rest for heart and soul that he has created. From every burden, from every anxiety, from all dread of shame or loss, even loss of love itself, that yoke will set us free."[9]

Another point that pervades MacDonald's writings is that we can obey God even while doubting. The doing of God's will tends to precede increased faith and trust in him:

---

4. "Life" in *Unspoken Sermons,* ser. 2.
5. "Self-Denial" in *Unspoken Sermons,* ser. 2.
6. "Truth" in *Unspoken Sermons,* ser. 3.
7. *Miracles of Our Lord,* ch. 4.
8. *Lilith,* ch. 39.
9. "Yoke of Jesus" in *Hope of the Gospel.*

Good and Not Evil Is the Universe

- "The faith required of us is faith in a person, and not in the truest of statements concerning anything, even concerning him; . . . faith in the living One, the very essence of it, consists in obedience to Him. A man can obey before he is sure, and except he obey the command he knows to be right, wherever it may come from, he will never be sure. To find the truth, man or woman must be true."[10]
- The soutar in *Salted with Fire* asserts, "Nane but them 'at follows whaur he leads, can ken that he verily is."[11]
- "Such a rough shaking of so-called faith, has been of endless service to many, chiefly by exposing the insecurity of all foundations of belief, save that which is discovered in digging with the spade of obedience."[12]
- "The more a man occupies himself in doing the works of the Father—the sort of thing the Father does, the easier will he find it to believe that such a Father is at work in the world."[13]
- "Obedience is the road to all things—the only way in which to grow able to trust [God]. Love and faith and obedience are sides of the same prism."[14]

Obedience to God's will begins with doing the thing that lies closest at hand, no matter how small it may seem: "The things readiest to be done, those which lie not at the door but on the very table of a man's mind, are not merely in general the most neglected, but even by the thoughtful man, the oftenest let alone, the oftenest postponed."[15] "We must learn to obey him in everything, and so must begin somewhere: let it be at once, and in the very next thing that lies at the door of our conscience!"[16] This imperative supersedes our moods, as the wise woman tells the princess in *A Double*

---

10. *Elect Lady*, ch. 30.
11. *Salted with Fire*, ch. 8.
12. *Paul Faber*, ch. 12.
13. *Paul Faber*, ch. 28.
14. *Donal Grant*, ch. 18.
15. "Cause of Spiritual Stupidity" in *Unspoken Sermons*, ser. 2.
16. "Truth in Jesus" in *Unspoken Sermons*, ser. 2.

The Primary Importance of Doing God's Will

Story: "Perhaps you will understand me better if I say it just comes to this, that you must *not do* what is wrong, however much you are inclined to do it, and you must *do* what is right, however much you are disinclined to do it."[17] This concept is also addressed in stanza 28 of "The Disciple" from *Poetical Works*, vol. 1.

Right and wrong do not need to be explained for us by anyone else, because God places the voice of conscience directly in each person, as the schoolmaster Graham states in *Malcolm*: "What he would have a man do, he lets him know in his mind."[18] Ranald Bannerman's father seems confident in his son's sense of right and wrong as he tells him, "My boy, do the will of God—that is, what you know or believe to be right, and fear nothing."[19] In *Hope of the Gospel* MacDonald explains that when doing God's will is difficult, God himself will provide the help we need. This help may be provided just in time, even when it's not clear beforehand how it could possibly occur.

When we obey God's will, we not only develop spiritually towards greater understanding and faith, but we also see God and become one with him:

> It is a beautiful thing to obey the rightful source of a command: it is a more beautiful thing to worship the radiant source of our light, and it is for the sake of obedient vision that our Lord commands us. For then our heart meets his: we see God.[20] For the *will* is the deepest, the strongest, the divinest thing in man; so, I presume, is it in God, for such we find it in Jesus Christ. Here, and here only, in the relation of the two wills, God's and his own, can a man come into vital contact—on the eternal idea, in no one-sided unity of completest dependence, but in willed harmony of dual oneness—with the All-in-all. When a man can and does entirely say, "Not my will, but thine be done"—when he so wills the will of God as to

---

17. *Double Story*, ch. 12.
18. *Malcolm*, ch. 69.
19. *Bannerman's Boyhood*, ch. 32.
20. "Love Thy Neighbour" in *Unspoken Sermons*, ser. 1.

do it, then is he one with God—one, as a true son with a true father.[21]

---

21. "Life" in *Unspoken Sermons*, ser. 2.

7

Spiritual Development: *An Infinite Progress*

The story of God's universe lies in the growth of the individual soul.[1]

A GRADUAL PROCESS

SPIRITUAL DEVELOPMENT IS A gradual process in which God is *pleased* with our beginning attempts but only *satisfied* with ultimate perfection. In *Unspoken Sermons* MacDonald has much to say about this gradual development:

- "[God] regards men not as they are merely, but as they shall be; not as they shall be merely, but as they are now growing, or capable of growing, towards that image after which he made them that they might grow to it. Therefore a thousand stages, each in itself all but valueless, are of inestimable worth as the necessary and connected gradations of an infinite progress."[2]
- "That no keeping but a perfect one will *satisfy* God, I hold with all my heart and strength; but that there is none else he cares for, is one of the lies of the enemy. What father is not pleased with the first tottering attempt of his little one to

---

1. *Heather and Snow*, ch. 3.
2. "Consuming Fire" in *Unspoken Sermons*, ser. 1.

walk? What father would be satisfied with anything but the manly step of the full-grown son?"[3]

- "We are the sons of God the moment we lift up our hearts, seeking to be sons—the moment we begin to cry *Father*. But as the world must be redeemed in a few men to begin with, so the soul is redeemed in a few of its thoughts and wants and ways, to begin with: it takes a long time to finish the new creation of this redemption.... So are we sons when we begin to cry Father, but we are far from perfected sons."[4]

- "Obedience is not perfection, but trying.... He knows that you can try, and that in your trying and failing he will be able to help you, until at length you shall do the will of God even as he does it himself. He takes the will in the imperfect deed, and makes the deed at last perfect."[5]

- "We may call a woman beautiful who is not perfect in beauty; in the Bible men are constantly recognized as righteous men who are far from perfectly righteous."[6]

- "[The Bible] demands of [any man] righteousness; when he yields that righteousness of which he is capable, content for the moment, it goes on to demand more: the common-sense of the Bible is lovely."[7]

FROM SLAVERY TO FREEDOM

Spiritual development is a transition from slavery to being a free, true child of God. Again turning to *Unspoken Sermons*, we read,

> [God] will have children, not slaves; but he may keep a slave in his house a long time in the hope of waking up the poor slavish nature to aspire to the sonship which

---

3. "Way" in *Unspoken Sermons*, ser. 2.
4. "Abba, Father!" in *Unspoken Sermons*, ser. 2.
5. "Truth in Jesus" in *Unspoken Sermons*, ser. 2.
6. "Righteousness" in *Unspoken Sermons*, ser. 3.
7. "Righteousness" in *Unspoken Sermons*, ser. 3.

belongs to him, which is his birthright. But the slave is not to be in the house for ever. The father is not bound to keep his son a slave because the foolish child prefers it. ... The real slave is he who does not seek to be a child; who does not desire to end his slavery; who looks upon the claim of the child as presumption; who cleaves to the traditional authorized service of forms and ceremonies, and does not know the will of him who made the seven stars and Orion, much less cares to obey it; who never lifts up his heart to cry "Father, what wouldst thou have me to do?" ... "Ye shall know the truth," the Lord says, "and the truth shall make you free. I am the truth, and you shall be free as I am free. To be free, you must be sons like me. To be free you must *be* that which you have to be, that which you are created. To be free you must give the answer of sons to the Father who calls you." ... The only free man, then, is he who is a child of the Father. He is a servant of all, but can be made the slave of none: he is a son of the lord of the universe. He is in himself, in virtue of his truth, free.[8]

DRIVEN BY OBEDIENCE

Spiritual development is a process driven by obedience to God's will: "[Abraham's faith] was that faith which is one with action: 'He went out, not knowing whither he went.' The very act of believing in God after such fashion that, when the time of action comes, the man will obey God, is the highest act, the deepest, loftiest righteousness of which man is capable, is at the root of all other righteousness, and the spirit of it will work till the man is perfect."[9] Writing about Hector's development in *Far Above Rubies*, MacDonald refers to "a stronger desire to do the will of the Father, which is surely the best thing God himself can kindle in the heart of any man. For what good is there in creation but the possibility

---

8. "Freedom" in *Unspoken Sermons*, ser. 3.
9. "Righteousness" in *Unspoken Sermons*, ser. 3.

of being yet further created? And what else is growth but more of the will of God?"[10]

UNDERSTANDING

Relative Unimportance

One aspect of spiritual development is an increased understanding. But MacDonald places little importance on intellectual understanding and suggests that we should not expect ourselves to understand perfectly. In *David Elginbrod* the tutor Hugh Sutherland explains to his tutee, "Why, Harry, to understand how God understands, you would need to be as wise as he is; so it is no use trying. . . . For my part, it would make me miserable to think that there was nothing but what I could understand. I should feel as if I had no room anywhere."[11] In *Salted with Fire*, the soutar asks his daughter, "Is God's wark wastit upo' you and me excep' we see intil't, and un'erstan't, Maggie?"[12] In *There and Back*, Barbara Wylder asserts: "One who never did anything we couldn't understand, couldn't be God."[13] In the same novel, MacDonald comments, "Truly the relation of the world to its maker cannot primarily be an intellectual one; it must be a relation tremendously deeper!"[14]

Preceded by Doing God's Will

MacDonald repeatedly argues that understanding must be preceded by obeying God's will. *Unspoken Sermons* addresses this principle many times:

- "It is to the man who is trying to live, to the man who is obedient to the word of the Master, that the word of the Master

10. *Far Above Rubies.*
11. *David Elginbrod*, bk. 2, ch. 4.
12. *Salted with Fire*, ch. 1.
13. *There and Back*, ch. 28.
14. *There and Back*, ch. 54.

unfolds itself. . . . For life, that is, action, is alone the human condition into which the light of the Living can penetrate."[15]

- "It was not for our understandings, but our will, that Christ came. He who does that which he sees, shall understand; he who is set upon understanding rather than doing, shall go on stumbling and mistaking and speaking foolishness. He has not that in him which can understand that kind. The gospel itself, and in it the parables of the Truth, are to be understood only by those who walk by what they find."[16]

- "[The parables] are for the understanding of that man only who is practical—who does the thing he knows, who seeks to understand vitally. They reveal to the live conscience, otherwise not to the keenest intellect."[17]

- "To the man who gives himself to the living Lord, every belief will necessarily come right; the Lord himself will see that his disciple believe aright concerning him."[18]

- "We may be sure also of this, that, if a man becomes the disciple of Christ, he will not leave him in ignorance as to what he has to believe; he shall know the truth of everything it is needful for him to understand. If we do what he tells us, his light will go up in our hearts."[19]

- "I only pray you to obey, and assert that thus only can you fit yourselves for understanding the mind of Christ. I say none but he who does right, can think right."[20]

- "Our business is not to think correctly, but to live truly; then first will there be a possibility of our thinking correctly."[21]

---

15. "Cause of Spiritual Stupidity" in *Unspoken Sermons*, ser. 2
16. "Last Farthing" in *Unspoken Sermons*, ser. 2.
17. "Last Farthing" in *Unspoken Sermons*, ser. 2.
18. "Truth in Jesus" in *Unspoken Sermons*, ser. 2.
19. "Truth in Jesus" in *Unspoken Sermons*, ser. 2.
20. "Truth in Jesus" in *Unspoken Sermons*, ser. 2.
21. "Justice" in *Unspoken Sermons*, ser. 3.

- "I believe that to him who obeys, and thus opens the doors of his heart to receive the eternal gift, God gives the spirit of his son, the spirit of himself, to be in him, and lead him to the understanding of all truth."[22]

- "He who is willing to do the will of the Father shall know the truth of the teaching of Jesus. The spirit is 'given to them that obey him.'"[23]

But MacDonald's assertion that obedience must come before understanding reaches far beyond *Unspoken Sermons*, finding expression in various other works of his:

- In *Annals of a Quiet Neighbourhood*, MacDonald points out that we can not begin to understand the Epistles in the New Testament until we obey what is taught in the Gospels.

- "He who acts right will soon think right; he who acts wrong will soon think wrong."[24] "The way to know is to do the known."[25]

- In *Mary Marston*, William Marston explains, "A Christian is just one that does what the Lord Jesus tells him. Neither more nor less than that makes a Christian. It is not even understanding the Lord Jesus that makes one a Christian. That makes one dear to the Father; but it is being a Christian, that is, doing what he tells us, that makes us understand him. Peter says the Holy Spirit is given to them that obey him: what else is that but just actually, really, doing what he says."[26] And in the same novel, Mary herself concurs: "The whole secret is to do the thing the Master tells you: then you will understand what he tells you."[27]

---

22. "Justice" in *Unspoken Sermons*, ser. 3.
23. "Light" in *Unspoken Sermons*, ser. 3.
24. *George and Michael*, vol. 2, ch. 34.
25. *George and Michael*, vol. 3, ch. 56.
26. *Mary Marston*, ch. 11.
27. *Mary Marston*, ch. 52.

Spiritual Development: An Infinite Progress

- This applies even to understanding oneself, according to Hester in *Weighed and Wanting*: "Perhaps if one tries to do right as things come up, one may get on without understanding oneself. I don't think, so far as I can make out, St. Paul understood himself always. Miss Dasomma says a great part of music is the agony of the musician after the understanding of himself. I will try to do what is right."[28]

- "Obedience alone holds wide the door for the entrance of the spirit of wisdom."[29]

- Adam in *Lilith* explains: "But to him who has once seen even a shadow only of the truth, and, even but hoping he has seen it when it is present no longer, tries to obey it—to him the real vision, the Truth himself, will come, and depart no more, but abide with him for ever."[30]

- In *Dish of Orts* MacDonald explains that spiritual development begins with obeying in the ways we know we should, which in turn leads us into understanding further truths. He goes on to say, "Concerning these words of [Christ's], [Jesus] says, or at least plainly implies, that only the obedient, childlike soul can understand them. . . . In respect of great truths investigation goes for little, speculation for nothing; if a man would know them, he must obey them. Their nature is such that the only door into them is obedience."[31]

- We read in "After Thomas Kempis" from *Poetical Works*:

    Gather wouldst thou the perfect grains,
    And Jesus fully understand?
    Thou must obey him with huge pains,
    And to God's will be as Christ's hand.[32]

---

28. *Weighed and Wanting*, ch. 30.
29. *Sir Gibbie*, ch. 38.
30. *Lilith*, ch. 43.
31. "Sketch of Individual Development" in *Dish of Orts*.
32. "After Thomas Kempis" in *Poetical Works*, vol. 1.

Preceded by Trust in God

Understanding must also be preceded by trust, as MacDonald sets forth in *Unspoken Sermons*. Taken in combination with the ideas presented above, this would suggest a necessary sequence of obedience, followed by trust, and finally understanding:

> He who trusts can understand; he whose mind is set at ease can discover a reason. How otherwise than by rebuking and quelling their anxiety, could those words have made [the disciples] see what then they saw? . . . The lesson [the Lord] would have had [the disciples] learn from the miracle, the natural lesson, the only lesson worthy of the miracle, was, that God cared for his children, and could, did, and would provide for their necessities. . . . The ground of the Master's upbraiding is not that they did not understand him, but that they did not trust God; that, after all they had seen, they yet troubled themselves about bread. Because we easily imagine ourselves in want, we imagine God ready to forsake us. . . . The moment their fear was taught to look up, that moment [the disciples] began to see what the former words of the Lord must have meant: their minds grew clear enough to receive and reflect in a measure their intent.[33]

Science and the Wisdom of the World

In discussing science and the wisdom of the world in *Unspoken Sermons*, MacDonald draws an important distinction by pointing out that "truth means more than fact, more than relation of facts or persons, more than loftiest abstraction of metaphysical entity—means being and life, will and action; for he says, 'I am the truth.'"[34] "The truth is God; the witness to the truth is Jesus. The kingdom of the truth is the hearts of men."[35] "I believe that every fact in nature is a revelation of God, is there such as it is because God is such as

---

33. "Cause of Spiritual Stupidity" in *Unspoken Sermons*, ser. 2.
34. "Truth" in *Unspoken Sermons*, ser. 3.
35. "Kingship" in *Unspoken Sermons*, ser. 3.

Spiritual Development: An Infinite Progress

he is; and I suspect that all its facts impress us so that we learn God unconsciously."[36]

Science has a limited interest in God's truth, as well as a limited ability to perceive it, as we read in *Unspoken Sermons*: "Things as they are, not as science deals with them, are the revelation of God to his children."[37] "Human science cannot discover God; for human science is but the backward undoing of the tapestry-web of God's science, works with its back to him, and is always leaving him—his intent, that is, his perfected work—behind it, always going farther and farther away from the point where his work culminates in revelation."[38] "The mere intellect can never find out that which owes its being to the heart supreme. The relation of the intellect to that which is born of the heart is an unreal except it be a humble one."[39] "The children of God must always be mocked by the children of the world, whether in the church or out of it—children with sharp ears and eyes, but dull hearts. Those that hold love the only good in the world, understand and smile at the world's children, and can do very well without anything they have got to tell them. In the higher state to which their love is leading them, they will speedily outstrip the men of science, for they have that which is at the root of science, that for the revealing of which God's science exists."[40]

MacDonald clearly placed a higher value on direct experiences of God's truth in nature than on the scientific study of facts: "I would not be supposed to depreciate the labours of science, but I say its discoveries are unspeakably less precious than the merest gifts of Nature, those which, from morning to night, we take unthinking from her hands."[41] In *England's Antiphon*, MacDonald

---

36. "Truth" in *Unspoken Sermons*, ser. 3.
37. "Truth" in *Unspoken Sermons*, ser. 3.
38. "Truth" in *Unspoken Sermons*, ser. 3.
39. "Truth" in *Unspoken Sermons*, ser. 3.
40. "Truth" in *Unspoken Sermons*, ser. 3.
41. "Voice of Job" in *Unspoken Sermons*, ser. 2.

decries "the present worship of science, and its refusal, if not denial, of all that cannot be proved in forms of the intellect."[42]

To those who would deny God's existence on the basis of science, MacDonald has a ready reply. "If a man tells me that science says God is not a likely being, I answer, Probably not—such as you, who have given your keen, admirable, enviable powers to the observation of outer things only, are capable of supposing him; but that the God I mean may not be the very heart of the lovely order you see so much better than I, you have given me no reason to fear. My God may be above and beyond and in all that."[43]

For more on this topic, see "The Yoke of Jesus" in *Hope of the Gospel*.

Adherence to Creed or Theology

MacDonald also places more importance on actively following Christ than on adherence to any creed or theology. He asserts that "to know Christ is an infinitely higher thing than to know all theology, all that is said about his person, or babbled about his work."[44] "It is not to follow him to take him in any way theoretically, to hold this or that theory about why he died, or wherein lay his atonement: such things can be revealed only to those who follow him in his active being and the principle of his life—who do as he did, live as he lived. There is no other following.... [A man] must follow no doctrine, be it as true as word of man could state it, but the living Truth, the Master himself."[45] "Thank God, we are nowise bound to accept any man's explanation of God's ways and God's doings, however good the man may be, if it do not commend itself to our conscience.... We must believe in the atoning Christ, and cannot possibly believe in any theory concerning the atonement."[46]

---

42. *England's Antiphon*, ch. 18.
43. *Miracles of Our Lord*, ch. 3.
44. "Voice of Job" in *Unspoken Sermons*, ser. 2.
45. "Self-Denial" in *Unspoken Sermons*, ser. 2.
46. "Truth in Jesus" in *Unspoken Sermons*, ser. 2.

Spiritual Development: An Infinite Progress

The narrator in *The Seaboard Parish* recounts that "the constant tendency to consider Christianity as associated of necessity with this or that form of it, instead of as simply obedience to Christ, had grown more and more repulsive to me as I had grown myself, for it always seemed like an insult to my brethren in Christ."[47] In *Sir Gibbie*, we are told that Janet had "no inclination to trouble Gibbie's heart with what men call the plan of salvation. It was enough to her to find that he followed her Master. Being in the light she understood the light, and had no need of system, either true or false, to explain it to her. She lived by the word proceeding out of the mouth of God. When life begins to speculate upon itself, I suspect it has begun to die."[48] And the title character of *Donal Grant* tells Lady Arctura, "Nothing but Christ himself, your lord and friend and brother, not all the doctrines about him, even if every one of them were true, can save you."[49]

Obeying God out of a belief *in* him is more important than believing the "right" things *about* him. In *The Elect Lady* Andrew says, "Right opinion, except it spring from obedience to the truth, is but so much rubbish on the golden floor of the temple."[50] In *A Rough Shaking* we read that:

> [Mr. Porson's] theories of religion were neither large nor lofty; he accepted those that were handed down to him, and did not trouble himself as to whether they were correct. He did what was better: he tried constantly to obey the law of God, whether he found it in the Bible or in his own heart. Thus he was greater in the kingdom of heaven than thousands that knew more, had better theories about God, and could talk much more fluently concerning religion than he. By obeying God he let God teach him. So his heart was always growing; and where the heart grows, there is no fear of the intellect; there it also grows, and in the best fashion of growth.[51]

47. *Seaboard Parish*, vol. 3, ch. 2.
48. *Sir Gibbie*, ch. 23.
49. *Donal Grant*, ch. 33.
50. *Elect Lady*, ch. 23.
51. *Rough Shaking*, ch. 6.

We need not adopt the doctrines pushed on us by others. "In Christ we must forget Paul and Apollos and Cephas, pope and bishop and pastor and presbyter, creed and interpretation and theory."[52] MacDonald describes a true believer as one "who will take his orders from the Lord himself, and not from other men claiming either knowledge or authority."[53]

MacDonald is generally critical of established theologies and churches. He especially rejects the misrepresentations of God that are promoted by religious authorities and the injuries that these misrepresentations inflict on unwitting people. In the "battle of the dead" that the narrator envisions in *Lilith*, "the holiest words went with the most hating blow."[54] In *Dish of Orts* MacDonald acknowledges that "religion has given more occasion of cruelty, as of all dishonesty and devilry, than any other object of human interest."[55]

In *Donal Grant*, MacDonald describes the contradictory theology that tortures Lady Arctura: "She tried to feel that she deserved to be burned in hell for ever and ever, and that it was boundlessly good of God—who made her so that she could not help being a sinner—to give her the least chance of escaping it. She tried to feel that, though she could not be saved without something which the God of perfect love could give her if he pleased, but might not please to give her, yet if she was not saved it would be all her own fault: and so ever the round of a great miserable treadmill of contradictions!"[56]

Neither church reformers nor their followers escape MacDonald's criticism. *David Elginbrod* contains the following remarks: "One grand aim of the reformers of the Scottish ecclesiastical modes appears to have been to keep the worship pure and the worshippers sincere by embodying the whole in the ugliest forms that could be associated with the name of Christianity." MacDonald then goes on to speak of the "degeneracy" of some followers

---

52. *Paul Faber*, ch. 31.
53. *There and Back*, ch. 40.
54. *Lilith*, ch. 11.
55. "Imagination: Its Function and Its Culture" in *Dish of Orts*.
56. *Donal Grant*, ch. 17.

Spiritual Development: An Infinite Progress

of these and other great reformers (naming Calvin specifically), which results as follows: "They take up what their leader, urged by the necessity of the time, spoke loudest, never heeding what he loved most; and then work the former out to a logical perdition of everything belonging to the latter."[57]

Misrepresentations of God

Many people are repelled by the cruel misrepresentations of God perpetrated by established religion: "The gospel according to this or that expounder of it, may repel [the child] unspeakably; the gospel according to Jesus Christ, attracts him supremely, and ever holds where it has drawn him. To the priest, the scribe, the elder, exclaiming against his self-sufficiency in refusing what they teach, he answers, 'It is life or death to me. Your gospel I cannot take. To believe as you would have me believe, would be to lose my God. Your God is no God to me. I do not desire him. I would rather die the death than believe in such a God. In the name of the true God, I cast your gospel from me; it is no gospel, and to believe it would be to wrong him in whom alone lies my hope.'"[58]

Speaking specifically of the poet Shelley, MacDonald says: "So far is he from being an opponent of Christianity properly so called, that one can hardly help feeling what a Christian he would have been, could he but have seen Christianity in any other way than through the traditional and practical misrepresentations of it which surrounded him. All his attacks on Christianity are, in reality, directed against evils to which the true doctrines of Christianity are more opposed than those of Shelley could possibly be. How far he was excusable in giving the name of Christianity to what he might have seen to be only a miserable perversion of it, is another question, and one which hardly admits of discussion here. It was in

---

57. *David Elginbrod*, bk. 1, ch. 8.
58. "Jesus and His Fellow Townsmen" in *Hope of the Gospel*.

the *name* of Christianity, however, that the worst injuries of which he had to complain were inflicted upon him."[59]

MacDonald hopes to present a true picture of Christ, rather than making this true image harder for others to see: "For myself, I take joyous refuge with the grand, simple, every-day humanity of the man I find in the story—the man with the heart like that of my father and my mother and my brothers and sisters. If I may but see and help to show him a little as he lived to show himself, and not as church talk and church ways and church ceremonies and church theories and church plans of salvation and church worldliness generally have obscured him for hundreds of years, and will yet obscure him for hundreds more!"[60]

Many people are unreceptive to the true image of Christ, as MacDonald laments in *Malcolm*: "It is much easier to persuade men that God cares for certain observances, than that he cares for simple honesty and truth and gentleness and loving-kindness."[61] But MacDonald's novels often feature characters who learn to care more for this true morality than the trappings of religion.

It is typical of MacDonald that he argues for a direct relationship with God, free of any distortions caused by intervening religious authorities. He asserts that "nothing claimed or taught, be the claimers or the teachers who they may, must come between the soul and the spirit of the father, who is himself the teacher of his children."[62] He argues that we must "follow Jesus, not as he is presented in the tradition of the elders, but as he is presented by himself, his apostles, and the spirit of truth."[63] "The babes must beware lest the wise and prudent come between them and the Father. They must yield no claim to authority over their belief, made by man or community, by church any more than by synagogue. That alone is for them to believe which the Lord reveals to their souls as true; that alone is it possible for them to believe with what he

59. "Shelley" in *Dish of Orts*.
60. *Mary Marston*, ch. 52.
61. *Malcolm*, ch. 48.
62. "Abba, Father!" in *Unspoken Sermons*, ser. 2.
63. "Self-Denial" in *Unspoken Sermons*, ser. 2.

counts belief. The divine object for which teacher or church exists, is the persuasion of the individual heart to come to Jesus, the spirit, to be taught what he alone can teach."[64]

MacDonald looks forward to the place where religion will be obsolete: "I *rejoice* to think that there will be neither church nor chapel in the high countries; yea, that there will be nothing there called religion, and no law but the perfect law of liberty. For how should there be law or religion where every throb of the heart says *God!* where every song-throat is eager with thanksgiving! where such a tumult of glad waters is for ever bursting from beneath the throne of God, the tears of the gladness of the universe! Religion? Where will be the room for it, when the essence of every thought must be God?"[65]

A RETURN TO A CHILDLIKE NATURE

Spiritual development can also be seen as a return to our true, original, childlike nature. This is not to be confused with childishness, as MacDonald explains: "There is a childhood into which we have to grow, just as there is a childhood which we must leave behind; a childlikeness which is the highest gain of humanity, and a childishness from which but few of those who are counted the wisest among men, have freed themselves in their imagined progress towards the reality of things."[66] "The real man is the divine idea of him; the man God had in view when he began to send him forth out of thought into thinking; the man he is now working to perfect by casting out what is not he, and developing what is he.... It is the original God-idea of the individual man that will at length be given, without spot or blemish, into the arms of love.... For the things which made him or her what he or she was, the things that rendered lovable, the things essential to the person, will be

---

64. "Yoke of Jesus" in *Hope of the Gospel.*
65. "Inheritance" in *Unspoken Sermons,* ser. 3.
66. *David Elginbrod,* bk. 1, ch. 6.

more present, because more developed."⁶⁷ In *Lilith* Mara tells the title character, "He will not change you; he will only restore you to what you were."⁶⁸

Being childlike is essential to understanding: "It is the heart of the child that alone can understand the Father."⁶⁹ "When the Lord took the little child in the presence of his disciples, and declared him his representative, he made him the representative of his father also; but the eternal child alone can reveal him. . . . [God] can be revealed only to the child; perfectly, to the pure child only. All the discipline of the world is to make men children, that God may be revealed to them. . . . The Son alone can reveal God; the child alone understand him."⁷⁰

Lilith contains numerous examples of MacDonald's admiration of the childlike characteristics of the "little ones," as well as references to the danger of growing out of this childlikeness in adulthood: "If a Little One doesn't care, he grows greedy, and then lazy, and then big, and then stupid, and then bad."⁷¹

THE DUNGEON OF SELF

Spiritual development also entails losing the focus on oneself. In fact MacDonald has much to say about what he calls "the dungeon of self." In *David Elginbrod* he speaks of "the only devil that can make hell itself a torture, the devil of selfishness—the only one that can possess a man and make himself his own living hell."⁷²

Many other works of MacDonald repeat this theme:

- "Self is but the shadow of life. When it is taken for life itself, and set as the man's centre, it becomes a live death in the man,

---

67. "Sorrow the Pledge of Joy" in *Hope of the Gospel*.
68. *Lilith*, ch. 39.
69. "Truth in Jesus" in *Unspoken Sermons*, ser. 2.
70. "Yoke of Jesus" in *Hope of the Gospel*.
71. *Lilith*, ch. 13.
72. *David Elginbrod*, bk. 3, ch. 12.

a devil he worships as his god."[73] "The man who lives a hunter after pleasure, not a labourer in the fields of duty, who thinks of himself as if he were alone on the earth, is in himself a lie."[74]

- "All love is a worship of the infinite: what is called a man's love for himself, is not love; it is but a phantastic resemblance of love; it is a creating of the finite, a creation of death. A man *cannot* love himself. If all love be not creation—as I think it is—it is at least the only thing in harmony with creation, and the love of oneself is its absolute opposite. I sickened at the sight of myself: how should I ever get rid of the demon?"[75]

- "Perhaps the worst devil a man can be possessed withal, is himself. In mere madness, the man is beside himself; but in this case he is inside himself; the presiding, indwelling, inspiring spirit of him is himself, and that is the hardest of all to cast out."[76]

- "Self simply makes devils of us. . . . Self is as full of worms as it can hold; God deliver us from it!"[77]

- "A man who lives to meditate upon and worship himself, is in the slime of hell."[78]

- "It is the bad that is in us that makes us think about ourselves."[79]

- "Self-importance is perhaps a yet deeper root of all evil than even the love of money."[80]

- "What a hell of horror, I thought, to wander alone, a bare existence never going out of itself, never widening its life

---

73. "Life" in *Unspoken Sermons*, ser. 2.
74. "Truth" in *Unspoken Sermons*, ser. 3.
75. *Wilfrid Cumbermede*, ch. 59.
76. *Mary Marston*, ch. 49.
77. *Donal Grant*, ch. 68.
78. *Home Again*, ch. 10.
79. "True Christian Ministering" in *Dish of Orts*.
80. *Far Above Rubies*.

in another life, but, bound with the cords of its poor peculiarities, lying an eternal prisoner in the dungeon of its own being!"[81]

Being in love with oneself is an inferior form of love. In *Salted with Fire* MacDonald describes James as being "in love with himself, and thereby shut out from the salvation of love to another."[82] And in *Heather and Snow*, he explains, "There is no more pitiable sight to lovers of their kind, or any more laughable to its haters, than two persons falling into the love rooted in self-love."[83]

So how are we to escape the dungeon of self? For MacDonald it seems to start with simply refusing to allow selfishness to direct our lives:

- "The self is given to us that we may sacrifice it; it is ours that we like Christ may have somewhat to offer—not that we should torment it, but that we should deny it; not that we should cross it, but that we should abandon it utterly: then it can no more be vexed. . . . It means this:—we must refuse, abandon, deny self altogether as a ruling, or determining, or originating element in us. It is to be no longer the regent of our action. We are no more to think, 'What should I like to do?' but 'What would the Living One have me do?'"[84]

- Addressing his own self, MacDonald says, "God is more to me than my consciousness of myself. He is my life; you are only so much of it as my poor half-made being can grasp—as much of it as I can now know at once. Because I have fooled and spoiled you, treated you as if you were indeed my own self, you have dwindled yourself and have lessened me, till I am ashamed of myself. If I were to mind what you say, I should soon be sick of you; even now I am ever and anon disgusted with your paltry, mean face, which I meet at every

---

81. *Lilith*, ch. 16.
82. *Salted with Fire*, ch. 3.
83. *Heather and Snow*, ch. 16.
84. "Self-Denial" in *Unspoken Sermons*, ser. 2.

Spiritual Development: An Infinite Progress

turn. No! let me have the company of the Perfect One, not of you! of my elder brother, the Living One! I will not make a friend of the mere shadow of my own being! Good-bye, Self! I deny you, and will do my best every day to leave you behind me."[85]

- "Although the idea of the denial of self is an entire and absolute one, yet the thing has to be done *daily*: we must keep on denying. It is a deeper and harder thing than any sole effort of most herculean will may finally effect."[86]
- Self-loathing is not the ultimate end of spiritual development, but a step along the path to forgetting oneself: "Self-loathing is not sorrow. Yet it is good, for it marks a step in the way home, and in the father's arms the prodigal forgets the self he abominates. Once with his father, he is to himself of no more account."[87]

Various characters in MacDonald's novels succeed in making this spiritual transformation. In *Salted with Fire*, for example, MacDonald writes of James Blatherwick: "Thus dwindled by degrees Blatherwick's self-reflection and self-seeking, and, growing divinely conscious, he grew at the same time divinely self-oblivious."[88]

Ultimately, however, it is God who provides the deliverance from the dungeon of self—both directly and through the presence of other people in our lives. "Self, accepted as the law of self, is the one demon-enemy of life; God is the only Saviour from it, and from all that is not God, for God is life, and all that is not God is death. Life is the destruction of death, of all that kills, of all that is of death's kind."[89] "Christ died to save us, not from suffering, but from ourselves."[90] "[The man with God's righteousness] does not take his joy from himself. He feels joy in himself, but it comes

---

85. "Self-Denial" in *Unspoken Sermons*, ser. 2.
86. "Self-Denial" in *Unspoken Sermons*, ser. 2.
87. *Lilith*, ch. 39.
88. *Salted with Fire*, ch. 26.
89. "Fear of God" in *Unspoken Sermons*, ser. 2.
90. "Freedom" in *Unspoken Sermons*, ser. 3.

to him from others, not from himself—from God first, and from somebody, anybody, everybody next."[91]

God provides others for us to love and thus escape the dungeon. "This love of our neighbour is the only door out of the dungeon of self."[92] "It is the lovely creatures God has made all around us, in them giving us himself, that, until we know him, save us from the frenzy of aloneness—for that aloneness is Self, Self, Self. The man who minds only himself must at last go mad if God did not interfere."[93] "For we are made for love, not for self. Our neighbour is our refuge; *self* is our demon-foe."[94]

Human interaction is essential to the development of the individual and the church. In *Lilith* MacDonald explains,

> No atmosphere will comfort or nourish his life, less divine than that offered by other souls; nowhere but in other lives can he breathe. Only by the reflex of other lives can he ripen his specialty, develop the idea of himself, the individuality that distinguishes him from every other. Were all men alike, each would still have an individuality, secured by his personal consciousness, but there would be small reason why there should be more than two or three such; while, for the development of the differences which make a large and lofty unity possible, and which alone can make millions into a church, an endless and measureless influence and reaction are indispensable. A man to be perfect—complete, that is, in having reached the spiritual condition of persistent and universal growth, which is the mode wherein he inherits the infinitude of his Father—must have the education of a world of fellow-men.[95]

In his typically hopeful fashion, MacDonald suggests that we can develop successfully despite the difficulty involved: "It is necessary for us, because there is bad in us, to think about ourselves,

---

91. "Righteousness" in *Unspoken Sermons*, ser. 3.
92. "Love Thy Neighbour" in *Unspoken Sermons*, ser. 1.
93. "Last Farthing" in *Unspoken Sermons*, ser. 2.
94. "Life" in *Unspoken Sermons*, ser. 2.
95. *Lilith*, ch. 18.

SPIRITUAL DEVELOPMENT: AN INFINITE PROGRESS

but as we go on we think less and less about ourselves, until at last we are possessed with the spirit of the truth, the spirit of the kingdom, and live in gladness and in peace. We are prouder of our brothers and sisters than of ourselves; we delight to look at them."[96]

HELPING OTHERS TO DEVELOP

How do we help others to develop spiritually? It does not involve forcing our own opinions, or even our own understanding of the truth, upon them, but advising them to act upon the truth that they already understand. If they do what they already know to be right, more of the truth will be revealed to them. "To let their light shine, not to force on them their interpretations of God's designs, is the duty of Christians towards their fellows."[97] And "let us remember that we are not here to convince men, but to let our light shine."[98]

AGING

MacDonald can also be expected to call attention to the positive developmental aspects of aging:

- "Who has not seen, as the infirmities of age grow upon old men, the haughty, self-reliant spirit that had neglected, if not despised the gentle ministrations of love, grow as it were a little scared, and begin to look about for some kindness; begin to return the warm pressure of the hand, and to submit to be waited upon by the anxiety of love? Not in weakness alone comes the second childhood upon men, but often in childlikeness. . . . The necessities of the old man prefigure and forerun the dawn of the immortal childhood. For is not our necessity towards God our highest blessedness—the fair cloud that hangs over the summit of existence? Thank God, he has made his children so noble and high that they cannot

---

96. "True Christian Ministering" in *Dish of Orts*.
97. "Truth in Jesus" in *Unspoken Sermons*, ser. 2.
98. "Sermon" in *Dish of Orts*.

- do without Him! I believe we are sent into this world just to find this out."[99]
- "The heart needs never be old. Indeed it should always be growing younger."[100]
- "Why should not a man be happy when he is growing old, so long as his faith strengthens the feeble knees which chiefly suffer in the process of going down the hill? True, the fever heat is over, and the oil burns more slowly in the lamp of life; but if there is less fervour, there is more pervading warmth; if less of fire, more of sunshine; there is less smoke and more light. Verily, youth is good, but old age is better—to the man who forsakes not his youth when his youth forsakes him."[101]
- "Let no man long back to the bliss of his youth—but forward to a bliss that shall swallow even that, and contain it, and be more than it. Our history moves in cycles, it is true, ever returning towards the point whence it started; but it is in the imperfect circles of a spiral it moves; it returns—but ever to a point above the former: even the second childhood, at which the fool jeers, is the better, the truer, the fuller childhood, growing strong to cast off altogether, with the husk of its own enveloping age, that of its family, its country, its world as well. Age is not all decay: it is the ripening, the swelling of the fresh life within, that withers and bursts the husk."[102]
- "But when weakness begins to show itself,—a shadow-background, against which the strength is known and outlined—when every movement begins to demand a distinct effort of the will, and the earthly house presses, a conscious weight, not upon its own parts only, but upon the spirit within, then indeed must a man *have* God, believe in him with an entireness independent of feeling, and going beyond all theory, or be devoured by despair. In the growing feebleness of old age,

---

99. *Adela Cathcart*, vol. 3, ch. 7.
100. *Seaboard Parish*, vol. 1, ch. 1.
101. *Seaboard Parish*, vol. 1, ch. 12.
102. *Marquis of Lossie*, ch. 40.

a man may well come to accept life only because it is the will of God; but the weakness of such a man is the matrix of a divine strength, whence a gladness unspeakable shall ere long be born—the life which it is God's intent to share with his children."[103]

- The passing of the years is not to be feared or hated, as it merely brings us closer to our return to God. This is the central theme of "Lycabas" from *Poetical Works*, vol. 2: The months of the passing year are not wolves after all, but shepherd dogs bringing us back to the Good Shepherd.

According to MacDonald, the ability to perceive God's presence in nature is a sign of advancing spiritual development:

> It was not always the solitude of her room that Mary sought to get out of the wind of the world. Her love of nature had been growing stronger, notably, from her father's death. If the world is God's, every true man ought to feel at home in it. Something is wrong if the calm of the summer night does not sink into the heart, for the peace of God is there embodied. Sometime is wrong in the man to whom the sunrise is not a divine glory for therein are embodied the truth, the simplicity, the might of the Maker. When all is true in us, we shall feel the visible presence of the Watchful and Loving; for the thing that he works is its sign and symbol, its clothing fact.[104]

Spiritual development entails moving beyond a preoccupation with heaven or hell, according to Thomas Wingfold, the curate in *Paul Faber, Surgeon*: "I know not one advanced Christian who tries to obey for the hope of Heaven or the fear of hell. Such ideas have long vanished from such a man. He loves God; he loves truth; he loves his fellow, and knows he must love him more."[105]

Spiritual growth never ends, as the title character of *Donal Grant* explains to Davie: "'Well, I don't think he will make me any

---

103. *Warlock o' Glenwarlock*, ch. 37.
104. *Mary Marston*, ch. 19.
105. *Paul Faber*, ch. 30.

Good and Not Evil Is the Universe

taller,' answered Donal. 'But the live part of me—the thing I love you with, the thing I think about God with, the thing I love poetry with, the thing I read the Bible with—that thing God keeps on making bigger and bigger. I do not know where it will stop, I only know where it will not stop. That thing is *me*, and God will keep on making it bigger to all eternity, though he has not even got it into the right shape yet.'"[106]

---

106. *Donal Grant*, ch. 18.

8

Faith: *To Mind What Christ Says to Us*

ACCORDING TO MACDONALD, TO mind what Christ says to us is "the beginning, middle, and end of faith."[1]

As we read in *Unspoken Sermons*, faith consists in obedience to God's will:

> Faith is that which, knowing the Lord's will, goes and does it; or, not knowing it, stands and waits, content in ignorance as in knowledge, because God wills. . . . The faith which will remove mountains is that confidence in God which comes from seeking nothing but his will.[2] Do you ask, "What is faith in him?" I answer, The leaving of your way, your objects, your self, and the taking of his and him; the leaving of your trust in men, in money, in opinion, in character, in atonement itself, *and doing as he tells you*. I can find no words strong enough to serve for the weight of this necessity—this obedience. . . . Get up, and do something the master tells you; so make yourself his disciple at once. Instead of asking yourself whether you believe or not, ask yourself whether you have this day done one thing because he said, Do it, or once abstained because he said, Do not do it. It is simply absurd

---

1. "Truth in Jesus" in *Unspoken Sermons*, ser. 2.
2. "Temptation in the Wilderness" in *Unspoken Sermons*, ser. 1.

to say you believe, or even want to believe in him, if you do not anything he tells you.[3]

Unspoken Sermons also distinguishes faith from understanding: "To hold a thing with the intellect, is not to believe it. A man's real belief is that which he lives by; and that which the man I mean lives by, is the love of God, and obedience to his law, so far as he has recognized it. . . . What a man believes, is the thing he does. . . . No manner or amount of belief *about him* is the faith of the New Testament."[4]

In keeping with John 20:29, MacDonald considers believing without seeing to be the strongest display of faith. Jesus's cry of "My God, my God, why hast thou forsaken me?" on the cross can be seen as the ultimate victory of faith at a time when Jesus himself could not see God:

> Never was God nearer him than now. For never was Jesus more divine. He could not see, could not feel him near; and yet it is "*My* God" that he cries. Thus the Will of Jesus, in the very moment when his faith seems about to yield, is finally triumphant. . . . It was a cry *in* desolation, but it came out of Faith. . . . God was his God yet. *My God*—and in the cry came forth the Victory, and all was over soon. Of the peace that followed that cry, the peace of a perfect soul, large as the universe, pure as light, ardent as life, victorious for God and his brethren, he himself alone can ever know the breadth and length, and depth and height. . . . In the sickness of this agony, the Will of Jesus arises perfect at last; and of itself, unsupported now, declares—a naked consciousness of misery hung in the waste darkness of the universe—declares for God, in defiance of pain, of death, of apathy, of self, of negation, of the blackness within and around it; calls aloud upon the vanished God. This is the Faith of the Son of God. God withdrew, as it were, that the perfect

---

3. "Truth in Jesus" in *Unspoken Sermons*, ser. 2.
4. "Truth in Jesus" in *Unspoken Sermons*, ser. 2.

Faith: To Mind What Christ Says to Us

Will of the Son might arise and go forth to find the Will of the Father.[5]

MacDonald continues in this vein: "But the highest condition of the Human Will, as distinct, not as separated from God, is when, not seeing God, not seeming to itself to grasp him at all, it yet holds him fast."[6]

God's indirect way of revealing himself is described in *Weighed and Wanting*: "Some people are constantly rubbing at their skylights, but if they do not keep their other windows clean also, there will not be much light in the house: God, like his body, the light, is all about us, and prefers to shine in upon us sideways: we could not endure the power of his vertical glory; no mortal man can see God and live; and he who loveth not his brother whom he hath seen, shall not love his God whom he hath not seen. He will come to us in the morning through the eyes of a child, when we have been gazing all night at the stars in vain."[7] And in *Salted with Fire* we read, "The Lord went away that they might believe in him when out of the sight of him, and so be in him, and he in them!"[8]

Mr. Raven reads the following verses to the narrator (Mr. Vane) in *Lilith*:

> But if I found a man that could believe
> In what he saw not, felt not, and yet knew,
> From him I should take substance, and receive
> Firmness and form relate to touch and view;
> Then should I clothe me in the likeness true
> Of that idea where his soul did cleave![9]

For MacDonald, imagination was not something relegated to the world of fantasy, but an essential means of expanding our belief to the greatest possible extent. He especially emphasizes

---

5. "Eloi" in *Unspoken Sermons*, ser. 1.
6. "Eloi" in *Unspoken Sermons*, ser. 1.
7. *Weighed and Wanting*, ch. 13.
8. *Salted with Fire*, ch. 4.
9. *Lilith*, ch. 29.

the role of imagination in extending faith beyond merely what is stated in Scripture. In *Unspoken Sermons* he asserts:

- "A man will please God better by believing some things that are not told him, than by confining his faith to those things that are expressly said—said to arouse in us the truth-seeing faculty, the spiritual desire, the prayer for the good things which God will give to them that ask him."[10]

- "What should I think of my child, if I found that he limited his faith in me and hope from me to the few promises he had heard me utter! The faith that limits itself to the promises of God, seems to me to partake of the paltry character of such a faith in my child—good enough for a Pagan, but for a Christian a miserable and wretched faith."[11]

- "Do you count it a great faith to believe what God has said? It seems to me, I repeat, a little faith, and, if alone, worthy of reproach. To believe what he has not said is faith indeed, and blessed. For that comes of believing in HIM. Can you not believe in God himself?"[12]

- "We know in whom we have believed, and we look for that which it hath not entered into the heart of man to conceive. Shall God's thoughts be surpassed by man's thoughts? God's giving by man's asking? God's creation by man's imagination? No. Let us climb to the height of our Alpine desires; let us leave them behind us and ascend the spear-pointed Himmalays of our aspirations; still shall we find the depth of God's sapphire above us; still shall we find the heavens higher than the earth, and his thoughts and his ways higher than our thoughts and our ways."[13]

---

10. "Higher Faith" in *Unspoken Sermons*, ser. 1.
11. "Higher Faith" in *Unspoken Sermons*, ser. 1.
12. "Higher Faith" in *Unspoken Sermons*, ser. 1.
13. "Higher Faith" in *Unspoken Sermons*, ser. 1.

FAITH: TO MIND WHAT CHRIST SAYS TO US

- "We must not let our poor knowledge limit our not so poor intellect, our intellect limit our faith, our faith limit our divine hope."[14]

MacDonald repeats this point in *The Seaboard Parish* and assures us that our imaginings can not go far astray when our intentions are good:

> The imagination is one of the most powerful of all the faculties for aiding the growth of truth in the mind.... If we do not thus employ our imagination on sacred things, [Jesus'] example can be of no use to us except in exactly corresponding circumstances—and when can such occur from one end to another of our lives? The very effort to think how he would have done, is a wonderful purifier of the conscience, and, even if the conclusion arrived at should not be correct from lack of sufficient knowledge of his character and principles, it will be better than any that can be arrived at without this inquiry.... Nor let anyone fear that such employment of the divine gift of imagination will lead to foolish vagaries and useless inventions; while the object is to discover the right way—the truth—there is little danger of that.[15]

This theme recurs in various other works of MacDonald: "And in the history of the world, the imagination has, I fancy, been quite as often right as the intellect, and the things in which it has been right, have been of much the greater importance."[16] "The imagination is that faculty which gives form to thought.... It is, therefore, that faculty in man which is likest to the prime operation of the power of God.... The imagination of man is made in the image of the imagination of God."[17] The imagination of man lives and moves and has its being in the imagination of God.

In *Salted with Fire* MacLear is upbraided by the minister, who challenges him to cite the Scripture upon which his imaginative

14. "Man's Difficulty Concerning Prayer" in *Unspoken Sermons*, ser. 2.
15. *Seaboard Parish*, vol. 1, ch. 7.
16. *Warlock o' Glenwarlock*, ch. 8.
17. "Imagination: Its Function and Its Culture" in *Dish of Orts*.

Good and Not Evil Is the Universe

ideas are based. "'Deed, sir, what scriptur hed I for takin my brakwast this mornin, or ony mornin? Yet I never luik for a judgment to fa' upon me for that! I'm thinkin we dee mair things in faith than we ken—but no eneuch! no eneuch!"[18]

Unspoken Sermons tells us that the truth is more than can be expressed in words, even the words of the Bible:

> Sad, indeed, would the whole matter be, if the Bible had told us *everything* God meant us to believe.... The Bible leads us to Jesus, the inexhaustible, the ever unfolding Revelation of God. It is Christ "in whom are hid all the treasures of wisdom and knowledge," not the Bible, save as leading to him.... The one use of the Bible is to make us look at Jesus, that through him we might know his Father and our Father, his God and our God. Till we thus know Him, let us hold the Bible dear as the moon of our darkness, by which we travel towards the east; not dear as the sun whence her light cometh, and towards which we haste, that, walking in the sun himself, we may no more need the mirror that reflected his absent brightness.[19] ... Words, being human, therefore but partially capable, could not absolutely contain or express what the Lord meant.... Seeing it could not give life, the letter should not be throned with power to kill; it should be but the handmaid to open the door of the truth to the mind that was *of* the truth.[20]

For MacDonald, even doubt can be construed in a positive way. His references to it are diverse in the exact points they make, but they share the element of hopefulness. In *Miracles of Our Lord*, MacDonald highlights the plea of the father in Mark 9:24:

> "Help thou mine unbelief." It is the very triumph of faith. The unbelief itself cast like any other care upon him who careth for us, is the highest exercise of belief. It is the greatest effort lying in the power of the man. No man can help doubt. The true man alone, that is, the faithful man,

---

18. *Salted with Fire*, ch. 1.
19. "Higher Faith" in *Unspoken Sermons*, ser. 1.
20. "Knowing of the Son" in *Unspoken Sermons*, ser. 3.

can appeal to the Truth to enable him to believe what is true, and refuse what is false. How this applies especially to our own time and the need of the living generations, is easy to see. Of all prayers it is the one for us.[21]

MacDonald also shares his positive view of doubt in various other works:

- "For a doubter is not without faith. The very fact that he doubts, shows that he has some faith. When I find anyone hard upon doubters, I always doubt the *quality* of his faith. It is of little use to have a great cable, if the hemp is so poor that it breaks like the painter of a boat. I have known people whose power of believing chiefly consisted in their incapacity for seeing difficulties. Of what fine sort a faith must be that is founded in stupidity, or far worse, in indifference to the truth and the mere desire to get out of hell! That is not a grand belief in the Son of God, the radiation of the Father."[22]

- In *Annals of a Quiet Neighbourhood*, the vicar comments, "A man may be on the way to the truth, just in virtue of his doubting."[23]

- Wynnie, the *Vicar's Daughter*, quotes her father as saying that "a true faith is like the Pool of Bethesda: it is when troubled that it shows its healing power."[24]

- "Every commonest day of his life, he who would be a live child of the living has to fight with the God-denying look of things, and believe that in spite of that look, seeming ever to assert that God has nothing to do with them, God has his own way—the best, the only, the live way, of being in everything, and taking his own pure, saving will in them.... Feelings are not scientific instruments for that which surrounds them; they but speak of themselves when they say, 'I am cold;

---

21. *Miracles of Our Lord*, ch. 7.
22. *Seaboard Parish*, vol. 3, ch. 10.
23. *Quiet Neighbourhood*, ch. 4.
24. *Vicar's Daughter*, ch. 31.

I am dark.' Perhaps the final perfection will be when our faith is utterly and absolutely independent of our feelings. I dare to imagine this the final victory of our Lord, when he followed the cry of *Why hast thou forsaken me?* with the words, *Father, into thy hands I commend my spirit*."[25]

- "If any one say that doubt can not coexist with faith, I answer, it can with love, and love is the greater of the two, yea, is the very heart of faith itself."[26]

- "A man may be haunted with doubts, and only grow thereby in faith. Doubts are the messengers of the Living One to rouse the honest. They are the first knock at our door of things that are not yet, but have to be, understood."[27]

- "Doubt must precede every deeper assurance; for uncertainties are what we first see when we look into a region hitherto unknown, unexplored, unannexed."[28]

- "For doubt will come, will ever come, / Though signs be perfect good, / Till heart to heart strike doubting dumb, / And both are understood."[29]

See also "Doubt Heralding Vision" from *Poetical Works*, vol. 2.

While some might find fear to be a sign of deficient faith, we can expect MacDonald to find a positive take on the concept, and he does not disappoint us. For one thing, he describes fear as a natural early stage in our relationship with God, before it is cast out by perfect love in accordance with 1 John 4:18: "Naturally the first emotion of man towards the being he calls God, but of whom he knows so little, is fear. . . . In him who does not know God, and must be anything but satisfied with himself, fear towards God is as reasonable as it is natural, and serves powerfully towards the development of his true humanity. . . . Fear is natural, and has a

---

25. *Warlock o' Glenwarlock*, ch. 36.
26. *Elect Lady*, ch. 32.
27. "Voice of Job" in *Unspoken Sermons*, ser. 2.
28. "Voice of Job" in *Unspoken Sermons*, ser. 2.
29. "Disciple" in *Poetical Works*, vol. 1.

part to perform nothing but itself could perform in the birth of the true humanity. Until love, which is the truth towards God, is able to cast out fear, it is well that fear should hold; it is a bond, however poor, between that which is and that which creates."[30]

"While they are such as they are, there is much in him that cannot but affright them; they ought, they do well to fear him. It is, while they remain what they are, the only true relation between them."[31] "When a child of God is afraid, it is a sign that the word *Father* is not yet freely fashioned by the child's spiritual mouth. The glory can breed terror only in him who is capable of being terrified by it; while he is such it is well the terror should be bred and maintained, until the man seek refuge from it in the only place where it is not—in the bosom of the glory."[32] "Until a man has love, it is well he should have fear."[33]

MacDonald also suggests that fear should not drive us away from God, but towards him:

> Yea, the fear of God will cause a man to flee, not from him, but from himself; not from him, but to him, the Father of himself, in terror lest he should do Him wrong or his neighbour wrong.[34] If then any child of the father finds that he is afraid before him, that the thought of God is a discomfort to him, or even a terror, let him make haste—let him not linger to put on any garment, but rush at once in his nakedness, a true child, for shelter from his own evil and God's terror, into the salvation of the Father's arms, the home whence he was sent that he might learn that it was home. What father being evil would it not win to see the child with whom he was vexed running to his embrace? how much more will not the Father of our spirits, who seeks nothing but his children themselves, receive him with open arms![35]

30. "Fear of God" in *Unspoken Sermons*, ser. 2.
31. "Fear of God" in *Unspoken Sermons*, ser. 2.
32. "Fear of God" in *Unspoken Sermons*, ser. 2.
33. *What's Mine's Mine*, vol. 1, ch. 11.
34. "Consuming Fire" in *Unspoken Sermons*, ser. 1.
35. "Fear of God" in *Unspoken Sermons*, ser. 2.

Nonetheless, perfect love must eventually cast out fear, as set forth in *Unspoken Sermons*: "We must forsake all our fears and distrusts for Christ."[36] "No being, for himself or for another, needs fear the light of God."[37] "In those then who believe that good is the one power, and that evil exists only because for a time it subserves, cannot help subserving the good, what place can there be for fear? The strong and the good are one; and if our hope coincides with that of God, if it is rooted in his will, what should we do but rejoice in the effulgent glory of the First and the Last?"[38] "So long as love is imperfect, there is room for torment. That love only which fills the heart—and nothing but love can fill any heart—is able to cast out fear, leaving no room for its presence."[39]

---

36. "Truth in Jesus" in *Unspoken Sermons*, ser. 2.
37. "Light" in *Unspoken Sermons*, ser. 3.
38. "Fear of God" in *Unspoken Sermons*, ser. 2.
39. "Fear of God" in *Unspoken Sermons*, ser. 2.

9

Hope:
Evermore Lifting Its Head and Rising Again

For MacDonald, hope needs no justification. In reference to Hector in *Far Above Rubies*, he says, "Once more his spirit rose upon the wave of a hope which he could neither logically justify nor dare to refuse; for hope is hope whencesoever it spring, and needs no justification of its self-existence or of its sudden marvelous birth. The very hope was in itself enough for itself."[1]

MacDonald suggests that small hopes should expand to the greatest possible extent. The short story "The Castle" tells metaphorically of our hope in Jesus's return, and concludes: "And the loftiest hope is the surest of being fulfilled."[2] "Ah, through what miseries are not even frail hopes our best and safest, our only *true* guides indeed, into other and yet fairer hopes!"[3] "That we do not know, is the best reason for hoping to the full extent God has made possible to us. If then we go wrong, it will be in the direction of the right, and with such aberration as will be easier to correct than what must come of refusing to imagine, and leaving the dullest traditional prepossessions to rule our hearts and minds, with no

---

1. *Far Above Rubies*.
2. "Castle" in *Portent and Other Stories*.
3. *Far Above Rubies*.

claim but the poverty of their expectation from the paternal riches. Those that hope little cannot grow much. To them the very glory of God must be a small thing, for their hope of it is so small as not to be worth rejoicing in."[4]

Hope should also determine our view of death, as MacDonald points out in *Hope of the Gospel*:

> If we do indeed expect better things to come, we must let our hope appear. A Christian who looks gloomy at the mention of death, still more, one who talks of his friends as if he had lost them, turns the bushel of his little-faith over the lamp of the Lord's light. Death is but our visible horizon, and our look ought always to be focussed beyond it. We should never talk as if death were the end of anything.... What light issues from such as make their faces long at the very name of death, and look and speak as if it were the end of all things and the worst of evils? Jesus told his men not to fear death; told them his friends should go to be with him; told them they should live in the house of his father and their father; and since then he has risen himself from the tomb, and gone to prepare a place for them.[5]

MacDonald further expounds on his hopeful view of death in *Alec Forbes*: "Death is not a breaker but a renewer of ties. And if in view of death we gird up the loins of our minds, and unite our hearts into a whole of love, and tenderness, and atonement, and forgiveness, then Death himself cannot be that thing of forlornness and loss."[6] This view is further articulated in *Wilfrid Cumbermede*: "I cannot greatly fear that which holds but the shadow of death. For what men call death, is but its shadow. Death never comes near us; it lies behind the back of God; he is between it and us."[7]

MacDonald assures us that hope will always exist: "Hope springs with us from God Himself, and, however down-beaten,

---

4. "Hope of the Universe" in *Hope of the Gospel*.
5. "Salt and the Light of the World" in *Hope of the Gospel*.
6. *Alec Forbes*, ch. 87.
7. *Wilfrid Cumbermede*, ch. 65.

Hope: Evermore Lifting Its Head and Rising Again

however sick and nigh unto death, will evermore lift its head and rise again."[8]

8. *Paul Faber*, ch. 31.

10

Love: *Active Kindness*

MacDonald emphasizes the essential importance of love: "The whole constitution of human society exists for the express end, I say, of teaching the two truths by which man lives, Love to God and Love to Man."[1] Love is our true essence: "Love, not hate, is deepest in what Love 'loved into being.'"[2]

MacDonald is obviously not unique in pointing out God's love for us. What *is* different here is that the concept of a loving God is not contradicted by MacDonald's other assertions. Put simply: reading MacDonald, it finally becomes possible to really believe in God's love for us. In *Adela Cathcart*, MacDonald writes approvingly of the curate Armstrong, who preached such that "all the sermon was a persuading of the people that God really loved them, without any *if* or *but*."[3] "God loves us always because he is our God . . . we live only by his love."[4] The central revelation to the disciples is "the eternal fact of God's love and care and compassion."[5] "[The miracle of feeding the crowd] had set forth to [the disciples] the truth of God's heart towards them; revealed the

1. "Love Thy Neighbour" in *Unspoken Sermons*, ser. 1.
2. *Lilith*, ch. 17.
3. *Adela Cathcart*, vol. 1, ch. 4.
4. "Eloi" in *Unspoken Sermons*, ser. 1.
5. "Cause of Spiritual Stupidity" in *Unspoken Sermons*, ser. 2.

Love: Active Kindness

loving care without which he would not be God. Had they learned this lesson, they would not have needed the reminder."[6]

For MacDonald, it is not only important to love our neighbor, but to let this love expand to the entire human race. This is emphasized in *Unspoken Sermons*; for example:

- "To refuse our neighbour love, is to do him the greatest wrong."[7]
- "The love that is more than law, and renders its breach impossible, lives in the endless story, coming out in active kindness."[8]
- "The love that enlarges not its borders, that is not ever spreading and including, and deepening, will contract, shrivel, decay, die."[9]
- "Thus will love spread and spread in wider and stronger pulses till the whole human race will be to the man sacredly lovely."[10]
- "[Man's] life is not in knowing that he lives, but in loving all forms of life. He is made for the All, for God, who is the All, is his life. And the essential joy of his life lies abroad in the liberty of the All."[11]
- "To be for one moment aware of such pure simple love towards but one of my fellows as I trust I shall one day have towards each, must of itself bring a sense of life such as the utmost effort of my imagination can but feebly shadow now—a mighty glory of consciousness!"[12]

---

6. "Cause of Spiritual Stupidity" in *Unspoken Sermons*, ser. 2.
7. "Love Thy Neighbour" in *Unspoken Sermons*, ser. 1.
8. "Love Thy Neighbour" in *Unspoken Sermons*, ser. 1.
9. "Love Thy Neighbour" in *Unspoken Sermons*, ser. 1.
10. "Love Thy Neighbour" in *Unspoken Sermons*, ser. 1.
11. "Love Thy Neighbour" in *Unspoken Sermons*, ser. 1.
12. "Life" in *Unspoken Sermons*, ser. 2.

- "There would be, even in that one love, in the simple purity of a single affection such as we were created to generate, and intended to cherish, towards all, an expansion of life inexpressible, unutterable."[13]
- "The one bliss, next to the love of God, is the love of our neighbour."[14]

In fact, the true heart loves all creatures of God's making:

- "Surely then, inasmuch as man is made in the image of God nothing less than a love in the image of God's love, all-embracing, quietly excusing, heartily commending, can constitute the blessedness of man; a love not insensible to that which is foreign to it, but overcoming it with good. Where man loves in his kind, even as God loves in His kind, then man is saved, then he has reached the unseen and eternal. . . . We must wait patiently for the completion of God's great harmony, and meantime love everywhere and as we can."[15]

---

13. "Life" in *Unspoken Sermons*, ser. 2.
14. "Self-Denial" in *Unspoken Sermons*, ser. 2.
15. "Browning's 'Christmas Eve'" in *Dish of Orts*.

11

Repentance, Forgiveness, and Salvation:
Reconciliation, the Only Satisfying Victory

IN VARIOUS WRITINGS, MACDONALD speaks of how God responds to our repentance: "Repentance once begun, however, may grow more and more rapid! If God once get a willing hold, if with but one finger he touch the man's self, swift as possibility will he draw him from the darkness into the light. For that for which the forlorn, self-ruined wretch was made, was to be a child of God, a partaker of the divine nature, an heir of God and joint heir with Christ."[1] In *Salted with Fire*, the soutar tells his daughter Maggie, "But whan man or wuman repents and heumbles himsel, there is He to lift them up, and that higher than ever they stede afore!"[2] Even when emphasizing man's role in repenting in the sense of "dismissing" or "sending away" his sins, MacDonald states that this will allow God to enter and take his place in his heart.[3]

Repentance is not once-and-done: even those of us "who have already repented, who have long ago begun to send away our sins, need fresh repentance every day."[4]

1. "Last Farthing" in *Unspoken Sermons*, ser. 2.
2. *Salted with Fire*, ch. 6.
3. "Remission of Sins" in *Hope of the Gospel*.
4. "Remission of Sins" in *Hope of the Gospel*.

MacDonald speaks convincingly of God's willingness to forgive us:

- "No amount of wrong-doing in a child can ever free a parent from the divine necessity of doing all he can to deliver his child; the bond between them cannot be broken."[5]

- "But few, perhaps no burdened souls can have any idea of the power that lies in God's forgiveness to relieve their consciousness of defilement. Those who say, 'Even God cannot destroy the fact!' care more about their own cursed shame than their Father's blessed truth! Such will rather excuse than confess. When a man heartily confesses, leaving excuse to God, the truth makes him free, he knows that the evil has gone from him, as a man knows that he is cured of his plague."[6]

- In *Salted with Fire*, the soutar reassures his daughter Maggie, "There's aye rain eneuch, as Maister Shaksper says, i' the sweet haivens to wash the vera han' o' murder as white as snow. The creatin hert is fu' o' sic rain."[7]

If we hope to be forgiven ourselves, we are bound to forgive others, as the Lord's Prayer suggests: "With our forgiveness to our neighbour, in flows the Consciousness of God's forgiveness to us; or even with the effort, we become capable of believing that God can forgive us."[8] "Forgiveness, as I have said, is not love merely, but love *conveyed as love* to the erring, so establishing peace towards God, and forgiveness towards our neighbour."[9] "He who is not perfect in forgiveness must be haunted; . . . he only is free whose love for the human is so strong that he can pardon the individual sin; he alone can pray the prayer, 'Forgive us our trespasses,' out of a full heart. Forgiveness is the only cure of wrong."[10]

---

5. "Voice of Job" in *Unspoken Sermons*, ser. 2.
6. *Donal Grant*, ch. 78.
7. *Salted with Fire*, ch. 6.
8. "It Shall Not Be Forgiven" in *Unspoken Sermons*, ser. 1.
9. "It Shall Not Be Forgiven" in *Unspoken Sermons*, ser. 1.
10. *Mary Marston*, ch. 4.

Repentance, Forgiveness, and Salvation

Love and forgiveness must be extended even to our enemies—in fact, even those who continue to wrong us. MacDonald addresses this topic with special thoroughness in *Unspoken Sermons*:

- "In a good man at least, 'revenge is,' as Lord Bacon says, 'a kind of wild justice,' and is easily satisfied. The heart's desire upon such a one's enemies is best met and granted when the hate is changed into love and compassion."[11]

- "It is in virtue of the divine essence which is in them, that pure essential humanity, that we call our enemies men and women. It is this humanity that we are to love—a something, I say, deeper altogether than and independent of the region of hate."[12]

- "Shall we leave our brother to his desolate fate? Shall we not rather say, 'With my love at least shalt thou be compassed about, for thou hast not thy own lovingness to infold thee; love shall come as near thee as it may; and when thine comes forth to meet mine, we shall be one in the indwelling God?'"[13]

- "Begin to love him now, and help him into the loveliness which is his. Do not hate him although you can."[14]

- "Whether [your neighbour] pay you what you count his debt or no, you will be compelled to pay him all you owe him. If you owe him a pound and he you a million, you must pay him the pound whether he pay you the million or not; there is no business-parallel here. If, owing you love, he gives you hate, you, owing him love, have yet to pay it."[15]

- "For the righteousness of God goes far beyond mere deeds, and requires of us love and helping mercy as our highest obligation and justice to our fellow men—those of them too

11. "Higher Faith" in *Unspoken Sermons*, ser. 1.
12. "Love Thine Enemy" in *Unspoken Sermons*, ser. 1.
13. "Love Thine Enemy" in *Unspoken Sermons*, ser. 1.
14. "Love Thine Enemy" in *Unspoken Sermons*, ser. 1.
15. "Last Farthing" in *Unspoken Sermons*, ser. 2.

who have done nothing for us, those even who have done us wrong."[16]

Reconciliation, and not revenge, is the only true victory over enemies: "Indeed there is that in the depths of every human breast which makes a reconciliation the only victory that can give true satisfaction."[17]

MacDonald also reminds us that we are not to judge others, but focus on making ourselves better: "What man can judge his neighbour aright save him whose love makes him refuse to judge him? Therefore are we told to love, and not judge. It is the sole justice of which we are capable, and that perfected will comprise all justice."[18] "Man is not made for justice from his fellow, but for love, which is greater than justice, and by including supersedes justice."[19] In *Alec Forbes of Howglen*, MacDonald tells us that Annie Anderson "was one of those simple creatures who perceive at once that if they are to set anything right for themselves or other people, they must begin with their own selves, their inward being and life."[20]

Numerous examples of characters who undergo spiritual improvement in the course of MacDonald's stories show that we should not give up on anyone, because no one is beyond hope.

MacDonald's remarks on salvation range from general to specific:

- According to Alister in *What's Mine's Mine*, "There is no salvation but to know God and grow like him."[21]
- The schoolmaster Graham in *Malcolm* explains salvation as follows: "No man can ever save his soul. God only can do that. You can glorify him by giving yourself up heart and soul

---

16. "Righteousness" in *Unspoken Sermons*, ser. 3.
17. *Alec Forbes*, ch. 24.
18. "Love Thy Neighbour" in *Unspoken Sermons*, ser. 1.
19. "Love Thine Enemy" in *Unspoken Sermons*, ser. 1.
20. *Alec Forbes*, ch. 26.
21. *What's Mine's Mine*, vol. 3, ch. 6.

Repentance, Forgiveness, and Salvation

and body and life to his Son. Then you shall *be* saved. *That* you must leave to *him*, and *do what he tells you*. There will be no fear of the saving then—though it's not an easy matter—even for *him*, as has been sorely proved."[22]

- "Then the road to eternal life is the keeping of the commandments! Had the Lord *not* said so, what man of common moral sense would ever dare say otherwise? What else can be the way into life but the doing of what the Lord of life tells the creatures he has made, and whom he would have live for ever, that they must do? It is the beginning of the way. If a man had kept all those commandments, yet would he not therefore have in him the life eternal; nevertheless, without keeping of the commandments there is no entering into life; the keeping of them is the path to the gate of life; it is not life, but it is the way—so much of the way to it. Nay, the keeping of the commandments, consciously or unconsciously, has closest and essential relation to eternal life."[23]

- Salvation requires a difficult process of spiritual development: "It always was, always will be, hard to enter into the kingdom of heaven. It is hard even to believe that one must be born from above—must pass into a new and unknown consciousness. The law-faithful Jew, the ceremonial Christian, shrinks from the self-annihilation, the Life of grace and truth, the upper air of heavenly delight, the all-embracing love that fills the law full and sets it aside. They cannot accept a condition of being as in itself eternal life. And hard to believe in, this life, this kingdom of God, this simplicity of absolute existence, is hard to enter."[24]

Although MacDonald is best known for embracing universalism and rejecting predestination, he discusses this directly in only a few places. In *David Elginbrod* MacDonald explains that the doctrine of election "in the Bible asserts the fact of God's choosing

---

22. *Malcolm*, ch. 53.
23. "Way" in *Unspoken Sermons*, ser. 2.
24. "Hardness of the Way" in *Unspoken Sermons*, ser. 2.

certain persons for the specific purpose of receiving first, and so communicating the gifts of his grace to the whole world," not "the choice of certain persons for ultimate salvation, to the exclusion of the rest."[25] In fact, the character Harry vehemently rejects this mistaken understanding of the doctrine, as MacDonald himself is said to have reacted to it when first presented with it.

Another rare example is found in *Adela Cathcart*, where the narrator John Smith overhears the cottager recounting his response to a sermon:

> And the man was telling them, sir, that God had picked out so many men, women, and children, to go right away to glory, and left the rest to be damned for ever and ever in hell. And I up and spoke to him; and "sir," says I, "if I was tould as how I was to pick out so many out o' my childeren, and take 'em with me to a fine house, and leave the rest to be burnt up i' the old one, which o' them would I choose?" "How can I tell?" says he. "No doubt," says I; "they aint your sons and darters. But I can. I wouldn't move a foot, sir, but I'd take my chance wi' the poor things. And, sir," says I, "we're all God's childeren; and which o' us is he to choose, and which is he to leave out? I don't believe he'd know a bit better how to choose one and leave another than I should, sir—that is, his heart wouldn't let him lose e'er a one o' us, or he'd be miserable for ever, as I should be, if I left one o' mine i' the fire."[26]

MacDonald pleads for our spiritual siblings in *Unspoken Sermons*, arguing that it would be impossible for us to be more loving towards these people than God is:

> Then indeed wilt thou be all in all. For then our poor brothers and sisters, every one—O God, we trust in thee, the Consuming Fire—shall have been burnt clean and brought home. For if their moans, myriads of ages away, would turn heaven for us into hell—shall a man be more merciful than God? Shall, of all his glories, his mercy

---

25. *David Elginbrod*, bk. 3, ch. 11.
26. *Adela Cathcart*, vol. 2, ch. 3.

alone not be infinite? Shall a brother love a brother more than The Father loves a son?"[27]

God is working even in the outer darkness, according to *Unspoken Sermons*: "The outer darkness is but the most dreadful form of the consuming fire—the fire without light—the darkness visible, the black flame. God hath withdrawn himself, but not lost his hold. His face is turned away, but his hand is laid upon him still. His heart has ceased to beat into the man's heart, but he keeps him alive by his fire. And that fire will go searching and burning on in him, as in the highest saint who is not yet pure as he is pure."[28] "God in the dark can make a man thirst for the light, who never in the light sought but the dark."[29]

What does MacDonald say about life after death? Brief glimpses, sometimes mere allusions to the "high countries," are scattered throughout his writings, but here are some specific remarks: "Whatever the place be like, one thing is certain, that there will be endless, infinite atonement, ever-growing love."[30] Eternal life can begin even before earthly death, as explained somewhat cryptically by Mr. Raven in *Lilith*: "Others had begun to die, that is to come alive, long before they came to us; and when such are indeed dead, that instant they will wake and leave us."[31]

One important aspect of life after death is the reunion with lost loved ones for all eternity. This thought must have been especially precious to MacDonald, a father who lost four children during his lifetime.

- "[God] will raise you from the dead, that I may behold you; that that which vanished from the earth may again stand forth, looking out of the same eyes of eternal love and truth, holding out the same mighty hand of brotherhood, the same

---

27. "Consuming Fire" in *Unspoken Sermons*, ser. 1.
28. "Consuming Fire" in *Unspoken Sermons*, ser. 1.
29. "Last Farthing" in *Unspoken Sermons*, ser. 2.
30. "Inheritance" in *Unspoken Sermons*, ser. 3.
31. *Lilith*, ch. 7.

delicate and gentle, yet strong hand of sisterhood, to me, this me that knew you and loved you in the days gone by."[32]

- "He who is the shepherd of the sheep will see that the sheep that love one another shall have their own again, in whatever different pastures they may feed for a time."[33]
- MacDonald also argues for such a reunion in his comments on the miracle of the resurrection in *The Miracles of Our Lord*.
- Even before his father's death, Cosmo imagines their reunion: "We shall meet again one day, and run at each other."[34]
- In *The Diary of an Old Soul*, MacDonald looks forward to his reunion with the daughter and son whom he had lost by this point in his life:

  » The entry for December 29:

  > Again I shall behold thee, daughter true;
  > The hour will come when I shall hold thee fast
  > In God's name, loving thee all through and through.
  > Somewhere in his grand thought this waits for us.
  > Then shall I see a smile not like thy last—
  > For that great thing which came when all was past,
  > Was not a smile, but God's peace glorious.[35]

  » The entry for December 30:

  > Twilight of the transfiguration-joy,
  > Gleam-faced, pure-eyed, strong-willed, high-hearted boy!
  > Hardly thy life clear forth of heaven was sent,
  > Ere it broke out into a smile, and went.
  > So swift thy growth, so true thy goalward bent,
  > Thou, child and sage inextricably blent,
  > Wilt one day teach thy father in some heavenly tent[36]

32. "God of the Living" in *Unspoken Sermons*, ser. 1.
33. "Displeasure of Jesus" in *Unspoken Sermons*, ser. 3.
34. *Warlock o' Glenwarlock*, ch. 18.
35. "December" in *Diary of Old Soul*.
36. "December" in *Diary of Old Soul*.

12

A General Disdain for Wealth and High Social Status: *The Power of This World*

WEALTH HAS NO BENEFICIAL effect on those who possess it: "Having never was, never could be well-being; . . . it is not by possessing we live, but by life we possess."¹ "The love of money has less in it to cure itself than any other wickedness into which wretched men can fall."²

In fact, it brings negative spiritual consequences with it:

- "Money is the power of this world—power for defeat and failure to him who holds it—a weakness to be overcome ere a man can be strong; . . . yea, to the redemption of those who have it, it is the saddest obstruction."³

- In *Gutta-Percha Willie*, MacDonald states that "even the wretched people who set their hearts on making money, begin by saving the first penny they can, and then the next and the next. And they have their reward: they get the riches they

---

1. "Hardness of the Way" in *Unspoken Sermons*, ser. 2.
2. *Adela Cathcart*, vol. 2, ch. 3.
3. "Way" in *Unspoken Sermons*, ser. 2.

want—with the loss of their souls to be sure, but that they did not think of."[4]

- The new king's obsession with accumulating gold ultimately leads to the collapse of Gwyntystorm in *The Princess and Curdie*.

- "There are many more generous persons among the poor than among the rich—a fact that might help some to understand how a rich man should find it hard to enter into the kingdom of heaven. It is hard for everybody, but harder for the rich. Men who strive to make money are unconsciously pulling instead of pushing at the heavy gate of the kingdom."[5]

What we have is meant to be shared, as it will be in heaven: "How would you not spend your money for the Lord, if He needed it at your hand! He does need it; for he that spends it upon the least of his fellows, spends it upon his Lord. To hold fast upon God with one hand, and open wide the other to your neighbor—that is religion; that is the law and the prophets, and the true way to all better things that are yet to come."[6] "Cleansed of greed, jealousy, vanity, pride, possession, all the thousand forms of the evil self, we shall be God's children on the hills and in the fields of that heaven, not one desiring to be before another, any more than to cast that other out; for ambition and hatred will then be seen to be one and the same spirit.—'What thou hast, I have; what thou desirest, I will; I give to myself ten times in giving once to thee. My want that thou mightst have, would be rich possession.'"[7]

For MacDonald, poverty is generally preferable to wealth and deserves at least equal respect:

- "Riches indubitably favour stupidity; poverty, where the heart is right, favours mental and moral development."[8]

---

4. *Gutta-Percha Willie*, ch. 23.
5. *Rough Shaking*, ch. 17.
6. *Paul Faber*, ch. 7.
7. "Cause of Spiritual Stupidity" in *Unspoken Sermons*, ser. 2.
8. *Warlock o' Glenwarlock*, ch. 9.

- In *There and Back*, MacDonald states that there is "not a word in the Bible against the poor, although a multitude of words against the rich. The sins of the poor are not once mentioned in the Bible, the sins of the rich very often. The rich may think this hard, but I state the fact, and do not much care what they think."[9]
- "[Francis] was dressed a little showily in a short coat of dark tartan, and a highland bonnet with a brooch and feather, and carried a lady's riding-whip—his mother's, no doubt—its top set with stones—so that his appearance was altogether a contrast to that of the girl [Kirsty]. She was a peasant, he a gentleman! Her bare head and yet more her bare feet emphasized the contrast. But which was by nature and in fact the superior, no one with the least insight could have doubted."[10]
- "To let our light shine, we must take care that we have no respect for riches: if we have none, there is no fear of our showing any. To treat the poor man with less attention or cordiality than the rich, is to show ourselves the servants of Mammon."[11]

MacDonald stops short of outright condemnation of the wealthy, however: "But with God all things are possible: He can save even the rich!"[12]

Active concern for the poor becomes the primary occupation of the title character of *Robert Falconer*, but the degenerate people of Bulika in *Lilith* have no such concern:

> "But there must be some poor!" I said.
> "I suppose there must be, but we never think of such people. When one goes poor, we forget him. That is how we keep rich. We mean to be rich always."[13]

---

9. *There and Back*, ch. 26.
10. *Heather and Snow*, ch. 3.
11. "Salt and the Light of the World" in *Hope of the Gospel*.
12. *Lilith*, ch. 39.
13. *Lilith*, ch. 23.

MacDonald's praise for humility and service to others is based on Christ's example: "For the idea of ruling was excluded where childlikeness was the one essential quality. It was to be no more who should rule, but who should serve. . . . What is the kingdom of Christ? A rule of love, of truth—a rule of service. The king is the chief servant in it. . . . So he that would be greatest among them, and come nearest to the King himself, must be the servant of all."[14] MacDonald reminds us that Christ came to serve, and that those who wish to be great must follow his example (e.g., in Matt 20:25–28). "It is not the ruling being who is most like God; it is the man who ministers to his fellow, who is like God."[15] "We cannot see the world as God means it, save in proportion as our souls are meek."[16]

MacDonald also advises us to be unconcerned with praise from others:

- "Whoever loves and cares himself for his appearance before the eyes of men, finds himself accused of paltry follies, stupidities, and indiscretions, and punished with paltry mortifications, chagrins, and anxieties. From such arraignment no man is free but him who walks in the perfect law of liberty—that is, the will of the Perfect—which alone is peace."[17]

- "From the faintest thought of the praise of men, we must turn away. No man can be the disciple of Christ and desire fame. To desire fame is ignoble; it is a beggarly greed. In the noble mind, it is the more of an infirmity. There is no aspiration in it—nothing but ambition. It is simply selfishness that would be proud if it could. Fame is the applause of the many, and the judgment of the many is foolish; therefore the greater the fame, the more is the foolishness that swells it, and the worse is the foolishness that longs after it."[18]

---

14. "Child in the Midst" in *Unspoken Sermons*, ser. 1.
15. "True Christian Ministering" in *Dish of Orts*.
16. "Heirs of Heaven and Earth" in *Hope of the Gospel*.
17. *Marquis of Lossie*, ch. 14.
18. "Right Hand and the Left" in *Hope of the Gospel*.

13

Nature as the Best Place to Worship: *Delighting in the Open Air*

THE PROTAGONISTS IN MACDONALD's stories often reflect his own preference for the temple of nature over the interior of church or chapel:

- In *David Elginbrod*, Maggie can only properly say her prayers in the wood: "I like places wi' green grass an' flowers amo't . . . whiles they gar me greet [make me cry] an' whiles they gar me lauch [make me laugh]; but there's mair i' them than that, an' i' the wood too. I canna richtly say my prayers in ony ither place."[1]
- "It is the temple of nature and not the temple of the church, the things made by the hands of God and not the things made by the hands of man, that afford the truest symbols of truth."[2]
- "For I always found the open air the most genial influence upon me for the production of religious feeling and thought. I had been led to try whether it might not be so with me by the fact that our Lord seemed so much to delight in the open air, and late in the day as well as early in the morning would

---

1. *David Elginbrod*, bk. 1, ch. 7.
2. *England's Antiphon*, ch. 13.

climb the mountain to be alone with His Father. I found that it helped to give a reality to everything that I thought about, if I only contemplated it under the high untroubled blue, with the lowly green beneath my feet, and the wind blowing on me to remind me of the Spirit that once moved on the face of the waters, bringing order out of disorder and light out of darkness, and was now seeking every day a fuller entrance into my heart, that there He might work the one will of the Father in heaven."[3]

---

3. *Quiet Neighbourhood*, ch. 13.

14

The Place of Animals in God's Kingdom: *Our Kindred*

MACDONALD REPEATEDLY ASSERTS THAT animals, as God's creatures, have their own place in his kingdom: "God is the God of the animals in a far lovelier way, I suspect, than many of us dare to think."[1] "The light of our life, our sole, eternal, and infinite joy, is simply God—God—God—nothing but God, and all his creatures in him. He is all and in all, and the children of the kingdom know it. He includes all things; not to be true to anything he has made is to be untrue to him."[2] "Your dog, your horse tells you about him who cares for all his creatures. None of them came from his hands. Perhaps the precious things of the earth, the coal and the diamonds, the iron and clay and gold, may be said to have come from his hands; but the live things come from his heart—from near the same region whence ourselves we came."[3]

This idea also occurs in the poem "A Hidden Life":

"God makes the beasts, and loves them dearly well—
Better than any parent loves his child,
It may be," would he say; for still the *may be*

---

1. "Last Farthing" in *Unspoken Sermons*, ser. 2.
2. "Righteousness" in *Unspoken Sermons*, ser. 3.
3. "Inheritance" in *Unspoken Sermons*, ser. 3.

Was sacred with him no less than the *is*—
"In such humility he lived and wrought—
Hence are they sacred. Sprung from God as we,
They are our brethren in a lower kind,
And in their face we see the human look."[4]

As such, MacDonald abhors cruelty towards animals, including harmful animal testing:

- "But now the lord of life has to look on at the wilful torture of multitudes of his creatures. It must be that offences come, but woe unto that man by whom they come! The Lord may seem not to heed, but he sees and knows."[5]

- Referring to our kinship with animals and frequent abuse of them, MacDonald says, "They are, in sense very real and divine, our kindred. If I call them our poor relations, it is to suggest that poor relations are often ill used."[6]

- "The higher your motive for [cruel animal testing], the greater is the blame of your unrighteousness. Must we congratulate you on such a love for your fellows as inspires you to wrong the weaker than they, those that are without helper against you? Shall we count the man worthy who, for the sake of his friend, robbed another man too feeble to protect himself, and too poor to punish his assailant? For the sake of your children, would you waylay a beggar? No real good can grow in the soil of injustice. . . . What man would he be who accepted the offer to be healed and kept alive by means which necessitated the torture of certain animals? Would he feel himself a gentleman—walking the earth with the sense that his life and conscious well-being were informed and upheld by the agonies of other lives?"[7]

---

4. "Hidden Life" in *Poetical Works*, vol. 1.
5. "Inheritance" in *Unspoken Sermons*, ser. 3.
6. "Hope of the Universe" in *Hope of the Gospel*.
7. "Hope of the Universe" in *Hope of the Gospel*.

The Place of Animals in God's Kingdom

- "There are women even who love dogs and dislike children; but, nauseous fact as this is, it is not so nauseous as the fact that there are men who believe in no animal rights, or in any God of the animals, and think we may do what we please with them, indulging at their cost an insane thirst after knowledge. Injustice may discover facts, but never truth."[8]

- How a person treats an animal is how they are likely to treat other people, as well: "Francie, Francie, i' the name o' yer father I beg ye to regaird the richts o' the neebour [i.e., the horse] ye sit upo'. Gien ye dinna that, ye'll come or lang to think little o' yer human neebour as weel, carin only for what ye get oot o' 'im!"[9]

- For more on this topic, see the sermon of the curate Thomas Wingfold in chapter 27 of *Paul Faber, Surgeon*.

MacDonald suggests that a higher state of spiritual development is required to truly know and understand animals: "The ways of God go into the depths yet unrevealed to us; he knows his horses and dogs as we cannot know them, because we are not yet pure sons of God."[10] In *Salted with Fire*, Isy asks her husband, "Div ye think, Jeames, that ever we'll be able to see inside thae doggies, and ken what they're thinkin?" He replies, "I wouldna won'er what we mayna come til; for ye ken Paul says, 'A' things are yours, and ye are Christ's, and Christ is God's!' Wha can tell but the vera herts o' the doggies may ae day lie bare and open to oor herts, as to the hert o' Him wi' whom they and we hae to do! Eh, but the thoughts o' a doggie maun be a won'erfu' sicht! And syne to think o' the thouchts o' Christ aboot that doggie! We'll ken them, I daurna weel doobt, some day! I'm surer aboot that nor aboot kennin the thouchts o' the doggie himsel!"[11]

---

8. *Rough Shaking*, ch. 1.
9. *Heather and Snow*, ch. 10.
10. "Inheritance" in *Unspoken Sermons*, ser. 3.
11. *Salted with Fire*, ch. 26.

Good and Not Evil Is the Universe

Perhaps MacDonald's most controversial assertion about animals is that they will enjoy eternal life along with us. This is discussed at great length in *Hope of the Gospel*:

> Would those Christians have me believe in a God who differentiates creatures from himself, only that they may be the prey of other creatures, or spend a few hours or years, helpless and lonely, speechless and without appeal, in merciless hands, then pass away into nothingness? I will not; in the name of Jesus, I will not. Had he not known something better, would he have said what he did about the father of men and the sparrows? . . . For what good, for what divine purpose is the maker of the sparrow present at its death, if he does not care what becomes of it? What is he there for, I repeat, if he have no care that it go well with his bird in its dying, that it be neither comfortless nor lost in the abyss? If his presence be no good to the sparrow, are you very sure what good it will be to you when your hour comes? Believe it is not by a little only that the heart of the universe is tenderer, more loving, more just and fair, than yours or mine. . . . I know of no reason why I should not look for the animals to rise again, in the same sense in which I hope myself to rise again—which is, to reappear, clothed with another and better form of life than before. If the Father will raise his children, why should he not also raise those whom he has taught his little ones to love?[12]

MacDonald addresses the topic in other works, as well. Speaking as *Wilfrid Cumbermede*, MacDonald recounts, "My uncle had, by no positive instruction, but by occasional observations, not one of which I can recall, generated in me a strong hope that the life of the lower animals was terminated at their death no more than our own. . . . I cannot see how the man who believes in soul at all, can say that the spirit of a man lives, and that the spirit of his horse dies."[13]

---

12. "Hope of the Universe" in *Hope of the Gospel*.
13. *Wilfrid Cumbermede*, ch. 21.

The Place of Animals in God's Kingdom

The curate Thomas Wingfold in *Paul Faber, Surgeon* says, "I count it as belonging to the smallness of our faith, to the poorness of our religion, to the rudimentary condition of our nature, that our sympathy with God's creatures is so small. Whatever the narrowness of our poverty-stricken, threadbare theories concerning them, whatever the inhospitality and exclusiveness of our mean pride towards them, we can not escape admitting that to them pain is pain, and comfort is comfort; that they hunger and thirst; that sleep restores and death delivers them: surely these are ground enough to the true heart wherefore it should love and cherish them—the heart at least that believes with St. Paul, that they need and have the salvation of Christ as well as we. Right grievously, though blindly, do they groan after it."[14]

To those indifferent to this topic, MacDonald says, "Has the question no interest for you? It would have much, had you now what you must one day have—a heart big enough to love any life God has thought fit to create. Had the Lord cared no more for what of his father's was lower than himself, than you do for what of your father's is lower than you, you would not now be looking for any sort of redemption."[15]

Animals may develop as well as humans: "The new heavens and the new earth in which dwell the sons of God, are to be inhabited by blessed animals also—inferior, but risen—and I think, yet to rise in continuous development."[16]

For more on this topic, see "Lessons for a Child" from *Poetical Works*, vol. 2.

---

14. *Paul Faber*, ch. 27.
15. "Hope of the Universe" in *Hope of the Gospel*.
16. "Hope of the Universe" in *Hope of the Gospel*.

15

Diversity: *Infinite and Lovable*

Diversity is in and from God. . . . in God's real men, that is, his ideal men, the diversity is infinite; he does not repeat his creations; every one of his children differs from every other, and in every one the diversity is lovable.[1]

The true heart loves all creatures of God's making:

> There are many, doubtless, who have not yet got farther in love than their own family; but there are others who have learned that for the true heart there is neither Frenchman nor Englishman, neither Jew nor Greek, neither white nor black—only the sons and daughters of God, only the brothers and sisters of the one elder brother. There may be some who have learned to love all the people of their own planet, but have not yet learned to look with patience upon those of Saturn or Mercury; while others there must be, who, wherever there is a creature of God's making, love each in its capacity for love—from the archangel before God's throne, to the creeping thing he may be compelled to destroy—from the man of this earth to the man of some system of worlds which no human telescope has yet brought within the ken of heaven-poring

---

1. "Sorrow the Pledge of Joy" in *Hope of the Gospel*.

sage. And to that it must come with every one of us, for not until then are we true men, true women—the children, that is, of him in whose image we are made.[2]

---

2. *Warlock o' Glenwarlock*, ch. 25.

Selected Works of George MacDonald

Adela Cathcart. Vol. 1. 1864. Project Gutenberg, 2005. Last updated August 8, 2012. https://www.gutenberg.org/ebooks/8892.

Adela Cathcart. Vol. 2. 1864. Produced by Jonathan Ingram et al. for Project Gutenberg, 2005. Last updated August 8, 2012. https://www.gutenberg.org/ebooks/8929.

Adela Cathcart. Vol. 3. 1864. Produced by Jonathan Ingram et al. for Project Gutenberg, 2005. Last updated August 8, 2012. https://www.gutenberg.org/ebooks/8943.

Alec Forbes of Howglen. 1865. Produced by John Bechard for Project Gutenberg, 2006. https://www.gutenberg.org/ebooks/18810.

Annals of a Quiet Neighbourhood. 1867. Produced by Charles Aldarondo et al. for Project Gutenberg, 2004. Last updated August 5, 2021. https://www.gutenberg.org/ebooks/5773.

At the Back of the North Wind. 1871. Produced by Martin Ward and David Widger for Project Gutenberg, 2008. Last updated August 7, 2019. https://www.gutenberg.org/ebooks/225.

A Book of Strife in the Form of the Diary of an Old Soul. 1880. Produced by John Bechard and David Widger for Project Gutenberg, 1999. Last updated January 17, 2013. https://www.gutenberg.org/ebooks/1953.

Cross Purposes and the Shadows. 1890. Produced by John Bechard for Project Gutenberg, 2006. https://www.gutenberg.org/ebooks/18859.

David Elginbrod. 1863. Produced by John Bechard and David Widger for Project Gutenberg, 2000. Last updated April 12, 2025. https://www.gutenberg.org/ebooks/2291.

A Dish of Orts: Chiefly Papers on the Imagination, and on Shakespeare. 1863. Produced by Jonathan Ingram et al. for Project Gutenberg, 2005. Last updated February 25, 2021. https://www.gutenberg.org/ebooks/9393.

Donal Grant. 1883. Produced by John Bechard et al. for Project Gutenberg, 2000. Last updated December 10, 2022. https://www.gutenberg.org/ebooks/2433.

A Double Story. 1875. Produced by Charles Aldarondo and Al Haines for Project Gutenberg, 2004. Last updated April 8, 2021. https://www.gutenberg.org/ebooks/5676.

The Elect Lady. 1888. Produced by Jonathan Ingram et al. for Project Gutenberg, 2005. Last updated February 25, 2021. https://www.gutenberg.org/ebooks/8944.

England's Antiphon. 1868. Produced by Jonathan Ingram et al. for Project Gutenberg, 2003. Last updated October 28, 2024. https://www.gutenberg.org/ebooks/10375.

Far Above Rubies. 1898. Produced by David Garcia et al. for Project Gutenberg, 2005. Last updated June 11, 2023. https://www.gutenberg.org/ebooks/8955.

The Flight of the Shadow. 1888. Produced by Jonathan Ingram et al. for Project Gutenberg, 2005. Last updated January 28, 2021. https://www.gutenberg.org/ebooks/8902.

Guild Court: A London Story. 1868. Produced by Mary Glenn Krause et al. for Project Gutenberg, 2017. Last updated October 23, 2024. https://www.gutenberg.org/ebooks/56176.

Heather and Snow. 1893. Produced by Jonathan Ingram et al. for Project Gutenberg, 2005. Last updated August 3, 2022. https://www.gutenberg.org/ebooks/9155.

A Hidden Life and Other Poems. 1864. Produced by Tim Rowe et al. for Project Gutenberg, 2004. Last updated October 28, 2024. https://www.gutenberg.org/ebooks/10578.

The History of Gutta-Percha Willie: The Working Genius. 1873. Produced by Jonathan Ingram et al. for Project Gutenberg, 2003. Last updated October 28, 2024. https://www.gutenberg.org/ebooks/10093.

Home Again. 1887. Produced by Jonathan Ingram et al. for Project Gutenberg, 2005. Last updated February 25, 2021. https://www.gutenberg.org/ebooks/8924.

The Hope of the Gospel. 1892. Produced by Jonathan Ingram et al. for Project Gutenberg, 2004. Last updated October 28, 2024. https://www.gutenberg.org/ebooks/14453.

Lilith: A Romance. 1895. Produced by John Bechard and David Widger for Project Gutenberg, 1999. Last updated February 26, 2021. https://www.gutenberg.org/ebooks/1640.

Malcolm. 1874. Produced by Martin Robb and Lisa Wadsworth for Project Gutenberg, 2004. Last updated February 9, 2024. https://www.gutenberg.org/ebooks/7127.

The Marquis of Lossie. 1877. Produced by Martin Robb and Lisa Wadsworth for Project Gutenberg, 2004. Last updated June 2, 2024. https://www.gutenberg.org/ebooks/7174.

Mary Marston. 1881. Produced by Charles Aldarondo et al. for Project Gutenberg, 2005. Last updated December 26, 2020. https://www.gutenberg.org/ebooks/8201.

Selected Works of George MacDonald

Miracles of Our Lord. 1848. Produced by Jonathan Ingram et al. for Project Gutenberg, 2005. Last updated September 15, 2017. https://www.gutenberg.org/ebooks/9103.

Paul Faber, Surgeon. 1879. Produced by Jonathan Ingram et al. for Project Gutenberg, 2004. Last updated October 28, 2024. https://www.gutenberg.org/ebooks/12387.

Phantastes: A Faerie Romance for Men and Women. 1858. Produced by Mike Lough and David Widger for Project Gutenberg, 2008. Last updated May 6, 2021. https://www.gutenberg.org/ebooks/325.

The Poetical Works of George MacDonald in Two Volumes. Vol. 1. 1893. Produced by Jonathan Ingram et al. for Project Gutenberg, 2005. Last updated February 16, 2013. https://www.gutenberg.org/ebooks/9543.

The Poetical Works of George MacDonald in Two Volumes. Vol. 2. 1893. Produced by Jonathan Ingram et al. for Project Gutenberg, 2006. Last updated December 27, 2020. https://www.gutenberg.org/ebooks/9984.

The Portent and Other Stories. 1864. Produced by Jonathan Ingram et al. for Project Gutenberg, 2005. Last updated February 25, 2021. https://www.gutenberg.org/ebooks/8913.

The Princess and Curdie. 1883. Produced by Jo Churcher and Al Haines for Project Gutenberg, 1996. Last updated January 1, 2021. https://www.gutenberg.org/ebooks/709.

The Princess and the Goblin. Illustrated by Jessie Willcox Smith. 1872. Produced by Suzanne Shell et al. for Project Gutenberg, 2010. Last updated January 7, 2021. https://www.gutenberg.org/ebooks/34339.

Ranald Bannerman's Boyhood. Illustrated by Arthur Hughes and M. V. Wheelhouse. 1871. Produced by Jonathan Ingram et al. for Project Gutenberg, 2004. Last updated February 25, 2001. https://www.gutenberg.org/ebooks/9301.

Robert Falconer. 1868. Produced by John Bechard and David Widger for Project Gutenberg, 2001. Last updated February 26, 2021. https://www.gutenberg.org/ebooks/2561.

A Rough Shaking. 1888. Project Gutenberg, 2005. Last updated May 20, 2023. https://www.gutenberg.org/ebooks/8886.

Salted with Fire. 1893. Produced by Jonathan Ingram et al. for Project Gutenberg, 2005. Last updated August 7, 2022. https://www.gutenberg.org/ebooks/9154.

The Seaboard Parish. 1868. Produced by Charles Aldarondo et al. for Project Gutenberg, 2005. Last updated July 16, 2022. https://www.gutenberg.org/ebooks/8562.

Sir Gibbie. 1879. Produced by John Bechard et al. for Project Gutenberg, 2000. Last updated October 29, 2022. https://www.gutenberg.org/ebooks/2370.

Stephen Archer, and Other Tales. 1886. Produced by Jonathan Ingram et al. for Project Gutenberg, 2005. Last updated April 19, 2013. https://www.gutenberg.org/ebooks/9191.

St. George and St. Michael. 1876. Produced by Charles Aldarondo et al. for Project Gutenberg, 2004. Last updated June 21, 2011. https://www.gutenberg.org/ebooks/5753.

There and Back. 1891. Produced by David Widger et al. for Project Gutenberg, 2005. Last updated February 25, 2021. https://www.gutenberg.org/ebooks/8879.

Thomas Wingfold, Curate. 1876. Produced by Charles Franks et al. for Project Gutenberg, 2004. Last updated February 26, 2021. https://www.gutenberg.org/ebooks/5976.

Unspoken Sermons, Series I, II, and III. 1867–1889. Produced by Jonathan Ingram et al. for Project Gutenberg, 2005. Last updated March 22, 2015. https://www.gutenberg.org/ebooks/9057.

The Vicar's Daughter. 1871. Produced by Jonathan Ingram et al. for Project Gutenberg, 2005. Last updated July 28, 2022. https://www.gutenberg.org/ebooks/9471.

Warlock o' Glenwarlock: A Homely Romance. 1881. Produced by Robert Prince et al. for Project Gutenberg, 2004. Last updated September 8, 2022. https://www.gutenberg.org/ebooks/6364.

Weighed and Wanting. 1882. Produced by David Garcia et al. for Project Gutenberg, 2005. Last updated August 19, 2012. https://www.gutenberg.org/ebooks/9096.

What's Mine's Mine. 1886. Produced by Charles Aldarondo et al. for Project Gutenberg, 2004. Last updated January 26, 2013. https://www.gutenberg.org/ebooks/5969.

Wilfrid Cumbermede. 1872. Produced by Jonathan Ingram et al. for Project Gutenberg, 2005. Last updated February 25, 2021. https://www.gutenberg.org/ebooks/9183.

Subject Index

action, 35, 37, 40, 50
   must precede feeling, 23
   redemptive, 20
aging, positive aspects of, 53–55
animals
   continuous development of, 91
   eternal life of, 90–91
   place in God's kingdom, 87–91
   testing and cruelty, 88–89
   understanding requires spiritual development, 89

belief, 30, 37, 43, 46–47, 58–59, 62–63
   without seeing, 58–59
Bible, 34, 62, 77–78, 83
   purpose of, 62

childhood, 47–48
   distinguished from childishness, 47
   essential to understanding, 48
   second, 53–54
Christ, 43, 46, 57, 62, 84
   actively following, 37, 42
   bringing us back to our Father, 4–5
   example for us, 4
   meaning and purpose of his death, 5, 51
   miracles of healing, 12
   mission on earth, 3–4, 84
   model of obedience to Father's will, 28
   revealing the Father, 3–4, 12
   yoke of, 4
Christianity, 43–46
   misrepresentations of, 45–46
claim(s), 35
   our claims on God 7–9
conscience, 30–31, 37, 42, 61
   placed directly in each person, 31
creation, 6–10, 11, 29, 35–36, 49, 60
   culminating in joy, 7
   divine agony, 7
   implying dependence on God, 7–8
   through God's imagination, 6
   through God's love, 6–7
criticism, of established theologies and churches, 44–45

depression, vii, 23, 25
   alleviated by helping others, 23–24

Subject Index

depression (*continued*)
   alleviated by physical labor, 26
   alleviated by recognizing God as our father, 24
   God as our refuge, 25
   MacDonald's familiarity with, 20–21, 26–27
   more of life itself as remedy, 22–23
development, 64, 82, 91
   spiritual, 33–56, 77, 89
diversity, 92–93
doctrine, vii, 44–46, 77–78
   relatively unimportant, 42–43
doubt
   does not prevent obedience to God's will, 29–30
   positive aspects of, 62–64
dungeon of self, 48–50
   alleviated by helping others, 23–24
   deliverance from, 50–52

eternal life, 25, 29, 77, 79–80, 90
   and keeping of commandments, 77
evil, 21–22, 49, 65, 66, 74, 82
   hated and understood only by God, 17
   turned to good purposes, 18
   ultimately defeated by good, vii–viii
   why permitted by God, 16–18

fact(s), 20, 40–41, 89
   distinguished from truth, 40–41
faith, 9, 23, 31, 35, 54, 57–66
   believing without seeing, 58–59
   consisting in obedience to God's will, 30, 57–58
   distinguished from understanding, 58
   preceded by doing God's will, 29–30
   purest and strongest in depression, 25–26
   role of imagination in, 59–62
fear, 5, 8–9, 16, 31, 40, 55, 66, 68
   driving us toward God, 65
   early stage in relationship with God, 64–65
feeling(s), 20, 23, 25, 54, 63–64, 85
   must be preceded by action, 23
forgiveness, 5, 68
   God's nature, 2
   God's willingness to forgive, 74
   our obligation to forgive others, 74–76
freedom, 34–35
   to choose good or evil, 16–18
   obtained by obedience to God's will, 29

God
   active even in outer darkness, 79
   as a consuming fire, 2–3, 78–79
   encompassing both male and female elements, viii, 2
   importance of recognizing God as Father, 24
   individual's relationship with, 11–13
   as life itself, 3, 6, 25, 50, 51, 71,
   misconceptions of, 1, 44, 45
   nature of, 1–5

Subject Index

as one who reveals, 3–4
as refuge against depression, 25

hardship, 14–18
    purpose and benefits of, 15–16
heaven, 5, 20, 55, 77, 82
hope, 9, 19, 23, 26, 45, 61, 66, 67–69, 90
    needs no justification, 67
    no one is beyond, 76
    should determine our view of death, 68
    should expand, 67–68
    unending, 68–69
human interaction
    as deliverance from dungeon of self, 51–52
    essential to development of individual and church, 52
humility, 84, 88

imagination
    role in creation, 6
    role in expanding faith, 59–62

joy, 3, 71
    after sorrow, 19–27
    as everlasting, 19
    sources of, 52, 87
    as outcome of creation, 7
judging others, 76

kingdom, 12, 15, 40, 43, 53, 77, 82, 84
    animals' place in God's, 87–91

life after death. *See* eternal life
love, 70–72
    casts out fear, 64–66
    expanded to entire human race, 71–72
    God's love for us, 70–71
    for one's enemies, 75–76
    of oneself, 49, 50
    as our true essence, 70

mental illness, 21

nature, 15, 40–41
    as best place to worship, 85–86
    perceiving God's presence in, 55

obedience to God's will
    brings freedom from slavery, 29
    drives spiritual development, 35–36
    importance of, 28–32
    as the key of life, 28
    modeled by Christ, 28
    more important than doctrine, 43–44
    precedes faith and trust in God, 29–30
    precedes understanding, 36–39
    in things lying closest at hand, 30–31
    uniting us with God, 31–32
    as the way to life, 29

poor, 14–15, 82, 83
    concern for, 83
poverty, 16
    contrasted with wealth, 82–83
praise from others, lack of concern for, 84
prayer, 5, 10, 60, 74
    bold and fearless approach to, 8–9
    persistence in, 10
    seemingly unanswered, 9–10

Subject Index

reconciliation, as only true victory over enemies, 76
relationship with God, individual's, 8, 11–13, 46, 64
repentance, 5
   always remains necessary, 73
   how God responds to, 73
reunion with departed loved ones, 79–80

salvation, 43, 46, 50, 65, 76–79, 91
   requires difficult process of spiritual development, 77
science
   denial of God's existence, 42
   difference between fact and truth, 40–41
   less important than direct experience of nature, 41
   limited perception of God's truth, 41
service to others, 84
sharing, 82
social status, 83
sorrow, vii
   joy after, 19–27
   as temporary, 19
spiritual development, 33–56
   driven by obedience to God's will, 35–36
   entails losing focus on oneself, 48–51
   as a gradual process, 33–34
   helping others to develop, 53
   human interaction as essential to, 52
   leads to salvation, 77
   leads to understanding of animals, 89
   as a return to our childlike nature, 47–48
   as a transition from slavery to freedom, 34–35
   unending, 55–56
status, social, 83
suffering, 14–18
   disliked by God, 14
   purpose and benefits of, 15–16
   shared by God, 14
   sustained by God in, 15

truth
   distinguished from fact, 40–41
   as more than can be expressed in words, 62
trust, 3, 21
   preceded by obedience to God's will, 29–30
   precedes understanding, 40

understanding
   being childlike as essential to understanding, 48
   independent of adherence to creed or theology, 42–45
   preceded by doing God's will, 36–39
   preceded by trust, 40
   relative unimportance of, 36
universalism, 3, 77–79

victory of good over evil, vii–viii

wealth, 81–83
   negative consequences of, 81–82
   without beneficial effect, 81
white stone with new name, 12–13
will, importance of doing God's, 28–32

yoke of Christ, 4

Scripture Index

NEW TESTAMENT

Matthew
20:25–28   84

Mark
9:24   62

Luke   10

John
20:29   58

1 John
4:18   64

Revelation
2:17   12

www.ingramcontent.com/pod-product-compliance
Lightning Source LLC
Chambersburg PA
CBHW072200100426
42738CB00011BA/2484